S-the-ket

W9-AXH-655

JOURNEYS

Senior Author
William K. Durr

*Senior Coordinating
Author*
John J. Pikulski

Coordinating Authors
Rita M. Bean
J. David Cooper
Nicholas A. Glaser
M. Jean Greenlaw
Hugh Schoephoerster

Authors
Mary Lou Alsin
Kathryn Au
Rosalinda B. Barrera
Joseph E. Brzeinski
Ruth P. Bunyan

Jacqueline C. Comas
Frank X. Estrada
Robert L. Hillerich
Timothy G. Johnson
Pamela A. Mason

HOUGHTON MIFFLIN COMPANY   BOSTON

Atlanta   Dallas   Geneva, Illinois   Lawrenceville, New Jersey   Palo Alto   Toronto

Acknowledgments

For each of the selections listed below, grateful acknowledgment is made for permission to adapt and/or reprint original or copyrighted material, as follows:

"Annie and the Old One," adapted from *Annie and the Old One*, by Miska Miles. Copyright © 1971 by Miska Miles. Reprinted by permission of Little, Brown and Company.

"The Buried Treasure," from *The Buried Treasure*, as retold by Djemma Bider. Copyright © 1982 by Djemma Bider. Adapted and reprinted by permission of Dodd, Mead & Company, Inc.

"Brave Janet of Reachfar," from *Brave Janet Reachfar*, by Jane Duncan. Text Copyright © 1975 by Jane Duncan. Reprinted by permission of Ticknor & Fields/Clarion Books, a Houghton Mifflin Company, and Macmillan, London and Basingstoke.

"The Clue on the Porch" by Karen MacLeod. Copyright © 1982. Originally appeared in *Cricket* magazine. Adapted and reprinted by permission of the author.

The Emperor's Plum Tree, (entire text, play version) by Michelle Nikly. Adapted from the French Translation by Elizabeth Shub. Copyright © 1982 by Albin Michel Jeunesse. Translation Copyright © 1982 by William Morrow & Company, Inc. Reprinted by permission of Greenwillow Books (A Division of William Morrow & Company, Inc.).

Continued on page 382.

2

Contents

Magazine Two

Journeys
Magazine One

Contents

Stories

Owney,
the Traveling Dog

by Lynn Hall

**Owney is a shaggy little puppy who finds an
unusual home. How does he also become a
world-famous traveling dog?**

It was a cold, snowy evening, but the streets of Albany, New York, were crowded with carriages drawn by fine horses. Women in long skirts and men in top hats smiled and nodded to one another and called, "Happy Holidays!"

Through the lines of carriages came the post office wagon bringing large sacks of mail from the railroad station to the post office. Running along beneath the wagon was a shaggy little puppy. He had to run hard to keep up with the horses, but this place, under the wagon, was safe. It was the only safety the small brown puppy had found from the dangers of the busy city streets. The wagon also kept the snow off him, although he was already so cold and wet that it hardly mattered.

Worse than being cold and tired was being hungry. The hunger made the puppy weak, and after a while he fell. Part of him just wanted to lie there and give up, but the stronger part of him said NO. He got up and ran until he had caught up with the mail wagon and was once again running beneath it.

Then the wagon slowed down and went into a place that was dark, quiet, and warm! The wagon stopped, and so did the pup.

Soon there were people around the wagon. The puppy saw black boots, gray pants legs, and huge gray bags labeled U.S. MAIL.

When all the black boots were on one side of the wagon, the pup trotted out on the opposite side and climbed up onto the nearest gray sack, which was not as soft as it looked. In fact, it had bumps and corners sticking up everywhere, but the pup was too sleepy to care about comfort. It was warm here, and he didn't need to run any more.

The pup curled up and slept soundly until a sharp hunger pain in his stomach woke him. Hours had passed. His shaggy coat was dry now, and he was thoroughly warm. When he lifted his head, he discovered that someone had put a woolen scarf over him. He sat up and blinked in amazement.

The horses and wagon were gone, and he was in a large dim room that was filled with stacks of gray mailbags. Several people were working at tables, sorting mail.

Closer to the pup, two men sat eating sandwiches and watching him.

"He's awake," James said.

"It's about time," Buck answered. "I was beginning to worry. He's too young to be out in this sort of weather."

The pup didn't know what the words meant, but he knew the sound of kindness. And he very definitely knew the smell of food! He tumbled down the side of the sack, but landed running. He went to the nearest man, who gave him a crust of his sandwich.

"He's starving, the poor little pup," Buck said, giving the puppy the rest of his sandwich — meat and all.

"What can we do with him?" James asked. "We can't put him out on the streets. He'd never survive."

13

"Let's just keep him here," James suggested. "He can be our mascot. It won't take much to feed him, and he'll be good company, especially at night."

So the pup stayed on in the post office. Buck and James named their little mascot Owney, and they fixed a bed for him in a warm corner of the office. The bed was an empty mail sack, folded over. The other postal workers on the night shift soon discovered the pup and began bringing extra food in their dinner pails. Before long, the thin little pup was a plump and happy puppy with thirty fond owners.

By the time spring arrived in Albany, Owney was large enough, and curious enough, to go exploring. He wandered up and down all the streets near the post office. He spent a lot of time in the barn where the post office horses and wagons were kept.

One bright day in June, Owney came home from a visit to the barn. He wanted to have a nap, but he discovered that his bed had disappeared. He went to the corner where it had been and stood there, puzzled.

One of the postal workers saw him and said, "Sorry, Owney. We were short of mailbags for this afternoon's mail, and we had to use yours. I'll fix you another bed when I get a minute."

Owney didn't understand the words at all, so he turned around and trotted out into the loading area. The wagon for the afternoon mail stood by the loading dock, where two postal workers were loading the mailbags.

Owney stopped and stared up at the loaded mailbags for a moment. Then he leaped onto the dock and from there into the wagon.

The little dog climbed up, around, and over the gray mailbags until he found the one that was his. It was crammed with letters instead of folded flat, as it was supposed to be, but it was Owney's bed. He circled three times on his sack and then settled down for a nap.

Owney slept through the trip down the streets of Albany and woke up only when the wagon stopped at the railroad depot. Close beside the wagon was a freight car, one of more than a hundred cars that made up the long, long train.

No one noticed Owney when he jumped down. The pup trotted up and down the railway platform

and stared at the train. It was the biggest thing he had ever seen. Its wheels held faint smells from many distant places, and Owney grew almost dizzy with the excitement of it all.

He returned to the postal wagon just in time to see his own gray sack as it was tossed inside the freight car. Owney got a running start and jumped up into the car.

"Scram, you mutt!" someone shouted, but Owney just moved around the mailbags. The man was too busy to chase him. Owney found his sack and settled into a soft place on the top of it. Then something whistled, and with a *whoosh* and a *chug*, the train began to move.

Owney sat up, pleasantly surprised that he was going on another ride. The train clicked and clacked as it picked up speed.

The door of the mail car had been left partly open, and Owney slid down the pile of mailbags and sat beside the door. Things he had never seen before flashed past. He sniffed the animal smells, the green smells, and the earth smells. His shaggy head moved from side to side, faster and faster, as he tried to see everything that was whizzing past. His tail wagged faster and faster with excitement.

Suddenly someone was standing behind him. It was a stranger, but he wore the same gray uniform that Owney's other friends wore. So Owney gave him a wag and went back to watching through the door.

"Would you look here," the man said to another man, who was sorting mail at a table. "We've got ourselves a little passenger."

Through the rest of the long journey, the postal workers played with Owney and even shared their meals with him. It was just like being at home for Owney, except there was the additional excitement of the outdoors whizzing by.

Late that night, the train stopped, and the men began unloading the mailbags.

"What should we do about the dog?" one man asked.

The other man said, "We'd better send him back to Albany on the 2:15 train. He must belong to somebody there."

Then he wrote a note and fastened it to Owney's collar. The note said, "Your dog rode to Buffalo, New York, with us. We're sending him back." When the mail car of the southbound 2:15 was loaded and ready to depart for Albany, the man handed Owney to another postal worker.

"Be sure to put him off at Albany," he said.

At midmorning the next day, Owney rode into the Albany post office atop the load of incoming mail sacks.

At first he was glad to be back among his friends, but soon he began to think about the fun he had on that train trip.

One day before long, another wagon of mail went to the train depot. In the back were seventeen gray

mailbags and one small shaggy dog. The little dog had a gleam in his bright black eyes.

This time the train went south, then west. The journey took five days, but Owney wasn't worried. All around him were the familiar mail sacks and kind workers in postal uniforms. They shared their food with him, and sometimes they talked about him.

"That's Owney," one worker would say to another. "He's the mascot of the Albany office. They sent out telegrams to all the stations asking to have him sent back if we found him."

"How did he get in our mail car?" someone would ask in amazement.

"When we weren't looking, I guess. He just likes to ride trains. He was on the 8:10 out of Albany. They took him off at Cleveland, Ohio, and put him on the

northbound 3:08. They passed him on to us. We'll put him off at Rochester, New York, and the workers there will put him on the 9:19 back to Albany."

When he got back this time, Owney was even less content to stay at home. It was as though home was no longer just the Albany Post Office. Home was anywhere there were mail sacks and people in gray uniforms to take care of him.

His collar now carried a metal tag with Owney's name on it and the words, "Please return to Albany Post Office."

Although he couldn't know it, Owney's fame spread throughout every post office in the United States. Postal workers hoped to find him among the sacks whenever a load of mail came in. Each place that Owney went, the workers gave him a tag with the name of their post office on it.

Before long, Owney's collar was so heavy with tags that it made him tired to hold up his head. The collar brought him a lot of attention when people were around; but when he was alone, it was just too heavy to wear. So he learned to pull it off with his front paws. Then, when he felt the train slowing for a station, he worked his head back through the collar. As the door opened, he would jump down from the train in all his jingling glory.

One day a package arrived for Owney from the postmaster general of the United States. Inside was a beautiful harness made of soft leather. "For Owney's tags," the note said.

As the years passed, the harness held many tags. There were tags from as far north as Alaska and as far south as Mexico. There were tags from every state and Canada too. Back and forth across the nation, trains rattled and roared. From the crack in the mail

car door peered two bright black eyes in a shaggy face.

Late one summer evening, when Owney was seven years old, he was at home in Albany. Buck and James talked about Owney's travels as they ate their midnight supper.

"There's only one place Owney hasn't been," Buck said thoughtfully.

"Where's that?" asked James.

Buck looked up at James and slowly began to smile. "Around the world."

Three hours later, Owney was aboard the west-bound 3:50 train. On his back was a traveling packet with his blanket and a comb and brush. There was also a note that said, "Owney wants to go around the world."

Three days later, Owney woke from a nap and sniffed the air. Behind him was the city of Tacoma, Washington. Before him was the ocean, with its salt smells. Owney was lying on mailbags that were bouncing toward the gangplank of a huge ship.

The shaggy little dog jumped down and stared in amazement as the mail sacks disappeared into the ship. This was new to him, but the ship smelled of exciting places.

"Go ahead, Owney," encouraged the postal workers around him. "You're going for a boat ride this time instead of a train ride."

Owney gave one sassy bark and then trotted up the gangplank to the huge ship.

The days that followed were full and happy days for Owney. He ate delicious meals at the captain's table in the fancy dining room. He wandered up and down the decks and was patted and admired by the passengers. At night he slept in the mail room in the lower part of the ship, where he was comfortably surrounded by his mailbags and his gray-suited friends.

When the ship docked in Japan, huge crowds were waiting to welcome it. The captain stood holding Owney under one arm. Suddenly he said to the steward, "Look, here comes the ambassador. I telegraphed the newspapers that Owney was aboard. The emperor must have heard about him and sent the ambassador to greet him."

When the engines were finally still and the gangplank down, the ambassador came aboard.

He saw Owney in the captain's arms and said, "So this is the famous traveling dog from America." The ambassador held out toward Owney an important-looking paper. "We welcome you to Japan, traveling dog. We give you this honorary passport as a token of the friendship between my country and yours."

Similar honors awaited Owney in China and Singapore. Then he sailed through the Suez Canal to Port Said, Egypt, then to Gibraltar and the Azores, and finally across the Atlantic Ocean to New York. In New York, friendly hands put him on the swiftest train to Albany.

On a day in late December, Owney trotted into the Albany post office and leaped into Buck's welcoming arms. Owney had circled the world!

If Owney had been famous before, he was even more famous now. Photographers and reporters came from the big newspapers.

"What will happen to him next?" one reporter inquired. "Will he stay home?"

"Probably," Buck said. "Owney's not a young dog anymore."

The men laughed fondly and smiled down at Owney.

Two days later, a fast freight train whistled across the plains of Kansas. From the crack in the mail car door peered two bright black eyes.

Author

Lynn Hall knows a great deal about animals, especially dogs. She has worked with them in professional dog shows. She has also been a veterinarian's assistant.

In the middle of woods and hills in Iowa, she has her own kennels, where she raises show dogs. Ms. Hall has written over thirty books, all about animals.

Thinking It Over

Comprehension Questions

1. How did Owney come to find a home in the Albany Post Office?
2. How did Owney become a traveling dog?
3. What did Owney find exciting about trains?
4. Why do you think the postal workers liked finding Owney among the sacks when a load of mail came in?
5. How did the captain feel about having Owney aboard his ship?

Vocabulary

Use the words below in sentences that tell about Owney's travels.

train	**travel**	**city**
journey	**arrive**	**engine**
aboard	**depot**	**passenger**
station	**trip**	**return**

Now use some of the words in sentences that tell about your own travels or the travels of someone you know.

Writing Questions for an Interview

Pretend you are a newspaper reporter interviewing Buck about Owney's travels. Write a list of questions you would like to ask him. Then ask a friend to play the part of Buck. Together, act out the interview.

Travel

by Edna St. Vincent Millay

The railroad track is miles away,
　　And the day is loud with voices speaking,
Yet there isn't a train goes by all day
　　But I hear its whistle shrieking.

All night there isn't a train goes by,
　　Though the night is still for sleep and dreaming
But I see its cinders red on the sky,
　　And hear its engine steaming.

My heart is warm with the friends I make,
　　And better friends I'll not be knowing,
Yet there isn't a train I wouldn't take,
　　No matter where it's going.

Survey

Thinking about what you might learn before you read an article or chapter in a book is one thing you do when you study. A quick survey before you start to read can help you understand and remember the information better.

When you survey, you "look over" the title, the pictures, and other parts of an article or chapter.

Survey the Title and Pictures

Usually the **title,** or name, of an article or chapter in a book gives an idea of what you will be learning. When you read the title, you begin to think of some of the things you may already know about that subject.

You should look at the **pictures** before you begin to read. The pictures may be paintings, drawings, or photographs. Survey the pictures to see if they give you more ideas about what you will learn.

Sometimes pictures have a word or group of words under or beside them. These words are called **captions**. Captions name, or tell, what is in the picture. When you survey a picture, you should also read the caption.

Survey the Introduction and Headings

Often there are a few sentences or paragraphs at the beginning of an article or chapter that let you know something about what you will learn. Read the **introduction** to get a quick idea of what the article or chapter is about.

Articles and chapters may have **headings.** Headings are words that are printed in boldface type between paragraphs or groups of paragraphs. These headings tell you what you will read about in each part of the article or chapter. Read the headings as part of the survey.

Special Print

Sometimes you will see words in **boldface** or *italic* type in the middle of a paragraph. These are special words that are important to remember. Usually, the meaning of these words will be given in the same paragraph. You should learn the meaning of these special words so you can add to your vocabulary.

After you have made your survey, you are ready to go back to the beginning of the article or chapter and read it carefully.

Make a survey of the article below. Then answer the questions that follow it.

How Dogs Help People

The friendship between dogs and humans began many years ago. Dogs were probably the first animals tamed by people. They can be trained to do many things for people because they are smart and like to please.

A Labrador guides blind woman along street

Guard Dogs

Many dogs have been trained to be guard dogs. They are trained in schools. Guard dogs may **protect** homes, stores, or factories. They keep buildings very safe by patrolling them and frightening away burglars.

Guide Dogs

Some dogs can be trained to help **guide** people who are blind or cannot see well. For example, they may direct a blind person when crossing a street. The German shepherd is used most often for this job. Other dogs that have been used as guide dogs are the Labrador and the collie.

Hearing Ear Dogs

Dogs can also be trained to help people who are deaf or cannot hear well. These dogs are known as hearing ear dogs. Hearing ear dogs can **alert** a deaf person to a ringing doorbell. They also let a deaf person know when an alarm sounds to signal danger.

Pets

Most dogs are kept by people just to have their **friendship**. Dogs show much interest in people and act as though they like them very much. Dogs are loved by people of all ages. Any kind of dog may be kept as a pet. Pet dogs give much joy to their owners.

Questions

1. What did the title tell you?
2. What types of dogs will you learn about?
3. What other words did you notice? Why?
4. What did you learn from the picture and caption?

Skill Summary

- Survey means to "look over" before you read.

- The title, pictures, captions, introduction, headings, and words in special print are things you might survey.

- A survey helps you get ready to read so that you will understand and remember better what you read.

The Post Office

Your community provides you with many services. One important service it provides is **mail delivery.** The United States Postal Service delivers millions of letters and other mail every day.

Delivering the mail is a big job. In the past, runners, horseback riders, boats, and trains were used to deliver the mail. Delivery, however, was slow. Today, trucks and airplanes, as well as boats and trains, help speed your mail on its way.

Do you know what happens to your letter when you mail it?

Mail coach used in the past

A postal worker takes your letter and all the other mail out of the mailbox and puts it into a large bag. The worker then takes the large bags of mail to a post office by truck.

Mailing a Letter

From the time you drop a letter into a mailbox until the time it reaches its destination, your letter may be handled by as many as six machines and twenty-five people!

Sorting the Mail by Size

Mail is sorted, or put in order, first by size. It is put on large moving belts where postal workers separate letter-size mail from larger envelopes and packages.

Letter-size mail then goes through a **facer-canceler.**

Letter-size mail going through a facer-canceler

This machine turns the letters so that the stamps are all facing the same way. It then **cancels**, or marks, the stamps by printing black lines over them. The stamps are canceled so that they cannot be used again. The facer-canceler also puts **postmarks** on the envelopes. A postmark usually tells the city and state from which a letter was mailed, the date it was mailed, and whether it was received at the post office during the morning or the afternoon. It also includes a **ZIP code.**

Sorting the Mail by ZIP Code

After the mail is sorted by size and the stamps are canceled, it has to be sorted again — this time by **destination.** The destination is the place where the letter is going.

The **ZIP code** is important in telling where a letter is going. ZIP is short for "Zoning Improvement Plan." The map below shows that the country is divided into ten ZIP code regions. In which ZIP code region is your state?

Each of the five numbers in the ZIP code stands for a different place. The first number shows the **region,** or part, of the country where the letter is going.

The second two numbers in the ZIP code show the smaller postal area within the larger region. The last two numbers show the post

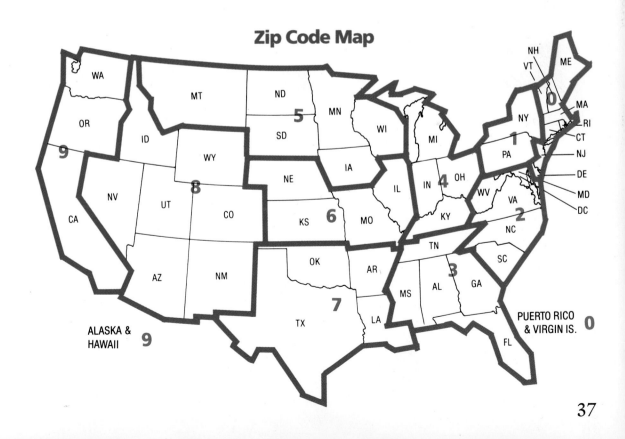

Zip Code Map

Postal worker keying ZIP code numbers into a ZIP mail translator

office or city to which the letter is to be delivered.

To sort the mail by destination, postal workers use a letter-sorting machine that has a computer called a **ZIP mail translator**. As the letter goes through the letter-sorting machine, a postal worker reads the ZIP code and keys into the ZIP mail translator the proper ZIP code numbers. This tells the computer the correct bin in which to put mail for a certain destination. Some post offices have automated letter-sorting machines with a more advanced computer called an **optical character reader.** This computer uses light to "read" the ZIP code.

Letters without ZIP codes have to be sorted by hand. This can really slow down delivery.

Delivering the Mail

Mail that is going a distance travels by truck, airplane, boat, or train. When the mail reaches its destination, it is taken to a post office where it is sorted again. This time the mail is sorted by *local* ZIP code, using the last two numbers in the ZIP code.

Letter carriers receive the mail that is going to the addresses along their **routes.** They sort the mail by address and put it into bundles by street or building. Then they arrange the bundles in their mailbags in the order in which they will deliver the mail.

Letter carrier delivering mail

Sometimes people send mail **special delivery**. Special delivery mail is taken by messenger from the post office directly to the person to whom it is addressed.

Other Postal Services

The post office provides services other than mail delivery. Some of these services are selling stamps and **money orders** and renting post office boxes. Stamps can be used to send mail or they can be collected. Money orders are a safe, easy way to send money in the mail. Post office boxes are often used by people who prefer to pick up their mail directly from the post office.

Even though machines have changed the way mail is sorted and have speeded up mail delivery, the job of the mail carrier remains the same. Mail carriers still deliver the mail to your home.

Questions

1. Where does a letter go after it is put into a mailbox? Use the diagram on page 41 to answer the question.
2. What three jobs does a facer-canceler do?
3. Why does the postal service cancel each stamp used?
4. What do the numbers in a ZIP code tell a postal worker?
5. Who brings the mail to your house or building?

Activity

Look at the map on page 37. Choose three ZIP code regions. Pretend that you have friends living in the regions you choose. Make up addresses for three of your friends. Be sure to include the ZIP codes in the addresses. Then write a letter to one of your friends.

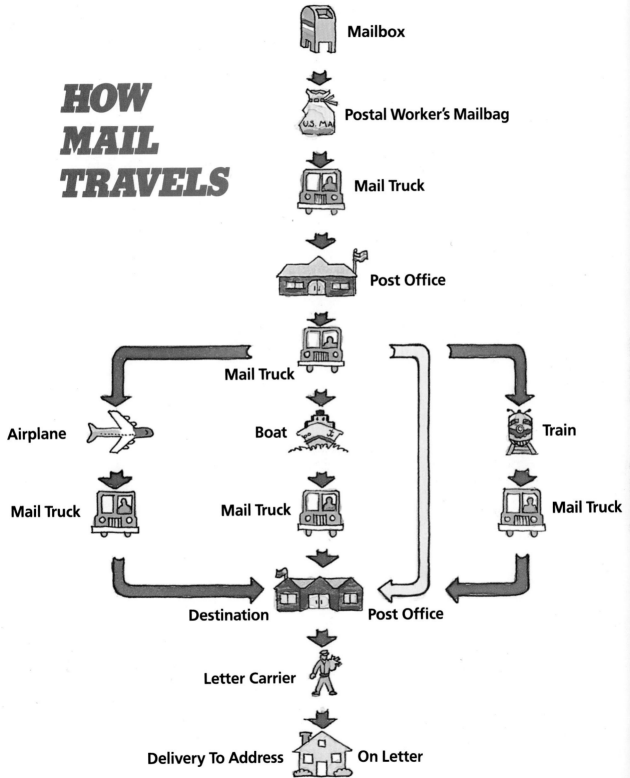

HOW MAIL TRAVELS

Mailbox

Postal Worker's Mailbag

Mail Truck

Post Office

Mail Truck

Airplane

Boat

Train

Mail Truck

Mail Truck

Mail Truck

Destination

Post Office

Letter Carrier

Delivery To Address

On Letter

41

Multiple-Meaning Words

I need a bat.

What kind of bat does the girl in the picture need? She certainly can't play ball with a bat that is an animal! She needs the kind of bat that is used to hit a ball. As you can see, the word *bat* has more than one meaning.

Many words have more than one meaning. When a word with more than one meaning appears in a sentence, use the context, or the sense of the other words, to figure out the meaning of that word.

Read the sentence with the word in boldface type. What is the meaning of *plate* in the sentence? Is it a dish for food? Or does it have something to do with baseball?

The batter struck out at the **plate.**

The words *batter* and *struck out* are clues that help you to figure out which meaning of *plate* is being used. Those words tell you that *plate* has something to do with baseball. The word *plate* in this sentence means "home base in the game of baseball."

Tell which meaning of the word in boldface type is used in each sentence below. Then give a sentence using the other meaning of the word.

1. Mr. White is the coach. He is going to **change** the game plan for today's game.
   a. make different
   b. small coins

2. The umpire said that Suzy was **safe** at first base.
   a. free from danger
   b. having reached a base without being put out

3. Todd was careful to keep one **foot** on the base.
   a. twelve inches
   b. end part of the leg

4. Tomorrow the coach will **pick** players for the baseball team.
   a. choose
   b. a sharp-pointed tool

Something Extra

Listen for words that have more than one meaning. You will hear your friends and your family say them. You will even hear yourself using them! Write the words in a notebook. Next to each word, write the sentence in which you heard the word used. Then write a second sentence that shows a different meaning for the word.

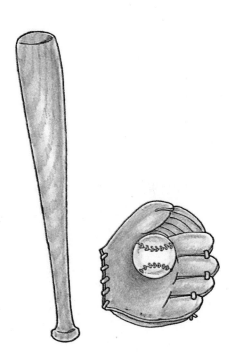

The Fastest Quitter in Town

by
Phyllis
Green

Johnny's friends think he's a quitter because
he never finishes a whole baseball game. Is
Johnny really a quitter?

The pitcher began the wind-up. He threw the ball to home plate. *Crack!* The batter hit a grounder. The shortstop scooped the ball up, and threw it to Johnny Colmer at first base.

"Easy out, Johnny," he yelled.

Johnny touched one foot on first base, ready to make the catch. He knew he had it! But the only thing he caught was . . . air!

Johnny threw down his mitt. "I quit!" he said.

Everybody started yelling, "You always quit when you do something stupid! Why don't you learn to catch?"

Johnny yelled back, "I *can* catch. Old Gromering can't throw."

"Come on. Let's play without him. We don't need him," someone said.

Johnny picked up his mitt and ran off the field. When he got to the edge of the schoolyard, he sat down on the bench.

Tears made paths down his dusty cheeks. He felt awful. He had promised himself that he would play the whole game today, but he had quit right at the start. If only he had been chosen for the other team. If only old Gromering knew how to throw a ball.

Johnny got up and wiped his face on his shirt. They would never let him back in the game. He decided to see Great-Grandfather and tell him about Gromering's bad throw.

Johnny Colmer lived with his parents at 1206 Fifth Street. His grandparents lived right next door.

Johnny's *great*-grandfather lived there too. He was ninety years old.

Great-Grandfather's eyes had become very bad. He could hardly see anything, but he had lots of good stories to tell. He told Johnny about the first automobiles, and about days when there was no television, and how nobody talked in the first movies.

When Johnny arrived, the first thing Great-Grandfather said was, "Short game today?"

Johnny didn't say anything.

"I thought you were going to play the whole game today. Something go wrong?" asked Great-Grandfather.

"Yeah," said Johnny.

"I see," Great-Grandfather said. "Well, do you suppose your grandmother has any snacks hidden away from us?"

It was hard for Great-Grandfather to get up, but Johnny helped him. Then Johnny got the fruit bowl from the top of the refrigerator.

"Get yourself some milk," Great-Grandfather said. "Then tell me about today. Someone break the rules?"

"No," Johnny said. "Just Joe Gromering. He thinks he's so hot. Only he never learned to throw a ball."

"That so?" said Great-Grandfather. "He's that bad, huh?"

"He's not *real* bad. Just throws a little high."

"That's why you quit? You missed the ball?"

"Not exactly. I mean, kind of. Well, tomorrow I'm going to play the whole game no matter what those stupid guys do."

Great-Grandfather patted his shoulder. "Tomorrow you'll be ready for him. Tomorrow you'll catch the ball. But Johnny, if by some chance you miss it, don't give up. Keep playing. It's a game. You're supposed to have fun."

The next afternoon, Johnny took his mitt. He walked over to the schoolyard. "Oh, no," everyone groaned. "Here comes Colmer, the fastest quitter in town."

Johnny stood around just hitting his mitt while the others played.

Finally one girl called, "All right, Colmer. We'll give you one more chance. Are you going to play the whole game today?"

"Yeah," said Johnny.

"Okay. Get out in left field."

In the third inning, when Johnny went to bat, he hit the ball far into center field. It looked like a homer. He ran fast. As he turned third base, he saw the ball moving toward the plate.

"Slide!" someone yelled.

He slid!

He got up smiling and brushed the dirt off his pants. He was sure he was safe by a hair.

"Out!" someone yelled.

"I'm safe!" Johnny shouted.

"You're out!" everyone yelled.

Johnny tried not to say anything, but suddenly the words came out.

"I quit."

Everybody began to scream and yell, "That was your last chance, Colmer. You're off the team for good. Don't come around ever again."

Johnny went straight to see Great-Grandfather, but he didn't tell him about the game because Great-Grandfather was very upset.

"What's the matter?" Johnny asked.

"Oh, Johnny," Great-Grandfather said, "I'm so glad you've come. I need your eyes. You know my ring, the gold one with the real diamond in the center? The one my dear Nancy gave me? She was

your great-grandmother, Johnny. And I've lost the ring she gave me."

"I'll find it," said Johnny.

Johnny crawled under Great-Grandfather's bed. He pulled up the pillow on his favorite chair. He looked through Great-Grandfather's pillowcase and sheets and blankets to see if the ring had fallen off his finger while he slept. He searched everywhere, and Great-Grandfather encouraged him.

"Look in the window seat, Johnny, and under the rug, and on the television table. It was just a small diamond, but it was real . . . a genuine diamond. And Nancy gave it to me."

But Johnny couldn't find it.

Johnny looked for the ring again the next day. He searched every day for a week, but he did not find it.

"I've got to find that ring, Johnny. I promised I'd never take it off, and now I've lost it."

"It's not your fault," Johnny said. "It must have fallen off. You can't help that."

Each day Great-Grandfather got more upset. Johnny's parents were very worried.

One day Mrs. Colmer said, "I bought a ring that looks just like his at the dime store. Johnny, give it to him. He can't see anything any more, and maybe he'll think it's his ring."

"But I can't," Johnny said. "He *will* know! He's not stupid. He wants the ring with the real diamond in it."

"Johnny, if we thought it would help, we would *buy* him a good ring with a little diamond in it. But he might lose it too."

"Okay," Johnny said, "but he'll know it isn't his ring."

Johnny went to see Great-Grandfather. He closed the door to the room so no one would hear. He put the ring in Great-Grandfather's hand.

"Johnny," he said, "that's not my ring."

"I know, Great-Grandpa, but Mom and Dad and Grandma and Grandpa are all upset because you're upset over losing the diamond ring. They want you to think this is your ring and to be happy again. Can you pretend it's your ring? And I promise if your ring can be found, I will find it. I will never give up."

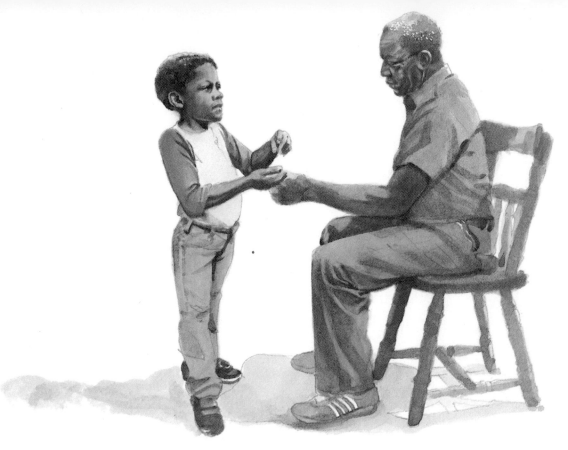

"Do you mean you won't quit on me? Okay, Johnny. I'll pretend."

For almost a month, Johnny didn't go near the schoolyard when his friends were playing ball. He was busy with his promise to Great-Grandfather. He searched and searched. Each day when he woke up, he always felt it would be the special day when he would find the ring.

But it never was.

One day when Johnny went to see him, Great-Grandfather said, "Johnny, I feel like a little sun. Help me out to the porch, will you?"

"You haven't been out for a long time, Great-Grandpa," said Johnny.

They sat on the porch together. Johnny looked at the back yard. "Great-Grandpa, were you out here on the day you lost your ring?"

Great-Grandfather bent his head to one side. "I don't know. It's hard to remember."

"Maybe you were. I've searched everywhere else."

Great-Grandfather got excited. "Johnny, sometimes when I'm out here, I walk over to the rock garden to touch the marigolds and zinnias. I can't see them too well, but I like to touch them and know they're there. Look over there, Johnny. I've got a feeling."

Johnny crawled through the grass, looking, looking. He came to the rock garden. He parted the marigolds and touched the earth around their stems. He felt around the edges of the rocks. He separated the red and yellow zinnias and looked through their leaves. He saw something near a zinnia stem — something shiny that sparkled in the sunlight.

"Great-Grandpa!" he yelled. "I found it!" He took the ring to his great-grandfather.

Tears came to the old man's eyes. He felt the lost ring. The little diamond was caked with dirt.

"You found my ring. Thank you, Johnny. I don't know what I would have done without you."

The whole family was thrilled. Johnny's grandmother put tape around the ring. Now it would fit Great-Grandfather's finger much better and not fall off again.

Johnny felt so good inside. It was such a good feeling to have found the ring. He hadn't given up. He hadn't even wanted to quit. The ring was so important to Great-Grandfather, he *never* would have quit.

The next day, he went around to the schoolyard. Everyone there laughed when they saw him. "Well, look who's here," they said.

"How about one more chance?" Johnny asked.

Everyone hooted and laughed. "For Colmer, the quitter?" they said.

Johnny smiled. "For Colmer, the fastest hitter in town," he said.

The girl at bat said, "I vote 'no' on the quitter. He was kicked out for good."

Someone else shouted, "No! He's a quitter."

But Gromering yelled, "C'mon, you guys. You know we need another player. Get over on third base, Johnny."

Johnny ran to third before they could change their minds.

It was after supper when he dropped in to see Great-Grandfather.

"Where have you been, Johnny? You're so late today. I thought you forgot about me."

"I was playing ball," said Johnny. "Can't you guess why I'm so late, Great-Grandpa?"

"Well, let's see," Great-Grandfather said, trying to remember.

"Great-Grandpa, I used to be a quitter! But today I didn't quit. And I feel great."

"You a quitter?" Great-Grandfather asked. "That doesn't seem possible. Not my Johnny. Let's go get a snack."

Johnny helped the old man into the kitchen. They ate fresh bread that Johnny's grandmother had made that day.

Great-Grandfather said, "You came late today. Where have you been?"

Johnny looked at his great-grandfather. He reached over and touched the lines in the old man's face. They were so deep. "I was playing baseball, Great-Grandpa."

"Did you win, Johnny?"

"No, we lost," Johnny said. "Boy, did we ever lose! The score was twenty to seven. But I got two home runs."

"I wish I could have seen you make those home runs. Well, I'm so tired, I better get to bed," Great-Grandfather said.

Johnny helped him back to his room.

"Good-night, Great-Grandpa," Johnny said. He kissed his forehead. "And thanks. Thanks a lot."

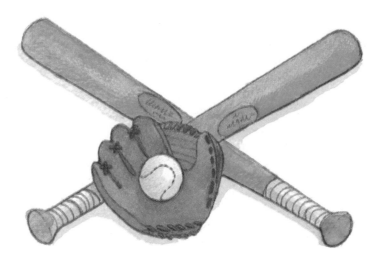

Author

The story you have just read was Phyllis Green's first book for children. She has written a number of books, as well as poems, short stories, and articles for magazines. *Gloomy Louie* is another of her books about a boy who plays baseball and meets problems in growing up.

Thinking It Over

Comprehension Questions

1. Why did everyone think Johnny was a quitter?
2. Why was Johnny able to spend a whole month looking for his great-grandfather's ring?
3. Why didn't Johnny quit when he couldn't find the ring?
4. Why do you think Johnny stopped being a quitter when he played baseball?
5. Why did Great-Grandfather say Johnny couldn't possibly be a quitter?

Vocabulary

Each word in the box below has more than one meaning. Use each word in a sentence to show one meaning. Then use the word in another sentence to show a different meaning.

bowl	pat	ring	play	base

Writing Paragraphs

Johnny's great-grandfather liked to tell stories about the days when he was young. Write about something that happened when you were younger.

Pronunciation Key

You know that you can use a **dictionary** or a **glossary** to find the meaning of a word. You can also use a dictionary or a glossary to find out how to pronounce a word.

Special Spelling

After each entry word in a dictionary or glossary, there is a **special spelling** to help you know what consonant and vowel sounds to use when you say the word. The letters in a special spelling may be quite different from the letters in the regular spelling of a word. If you use the sounds that the letters stand for in a special spelling, you will be able to say the word correctly.

Here is the way the words *ache, ruin,* and *avoid* might appear, without their meanings, in a dictionary:

ache (āk)   **ru·in** (r$\overline{oo}$′ĭn)   **a·void** (ə **void′**)

A word with more than one syllable is printed with dots to show where the word is broken into syllables. Beside the word is the special spelling.

The letters in the special spellings stand for the sounds you hear when the words *ache, ruin,* and *avoid* are pronounced. If you did not know how to pronounce those words, you would use the special spellings together with a pronunciation key.

Pronunciation Key

A **pronunciation key** is like a code to the pronunciation of a word. It helps you remember what the letters and marks in the special spelling mean. It comes at the bottom of one of two facing pages in most dictionaries and glossaries. The Glossary in this book uses the following pronunciation key:

ă pat/ ā pay/ â care/ ä father/ ĕ pet/ ē be/ ĭ pit/ ī pie/ î fierce/ ŏ pot/ ō go/ ô paw, for/ oi oil/ o͝o book/ o͞o boot/ ou out/ ŭ cut/ û fur/ *th* **th**e/ th **th**in/ hw **wh**ich/ zh vi**s**ion/ ə **a**go, it**e**m, penc**i**l, at**o**m, circ**u**s

The pronunciation key shows all the letters that you will find in a special spelling, except for most consonants. Consonants in special spellings stand for their usual sounds.

Beside each letter and mark in the pronunciation key you will find a word. That word gives you the vowel sound to use for that letter and mark. These words are called **key words.**

Notice that the letters for the *long vowel sounds* have a straight line over them: ā ē ī ō. If you say the key words beside those letters, you will hear the long vowel sound in each. In the special spelling of an entry word, the long *u* sound is shown like this: yo͞o.

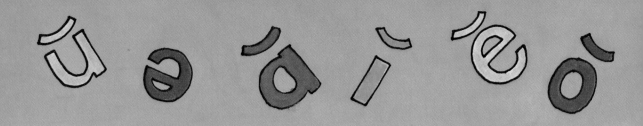

Letters for the *short vowel sounds* all have a curved line over them: ă ĕ ĭ ŏ ŭ. If you say the key words beside them, you will hear the short vowel sound in each.

Now find the mark in the pronunciation key that looks like this: ə. It is called a **schwa.** It stands for a sound that many different vowels may stand for. Say the words that follow it to yourself. You will hear that same vowel sound in each one. The letters a, e, i, o, and u may all stand for that same schwa sound.

Look at the special spelling for the word *ache.* To find the sound that ā stands for, look at the pronunciation key. You can see that the key word for that sound is p**ay**. This means that the ā in the special spelling stands for the sound for **ay** in p**ay** (the long *a* sound). After ā in the special spelling is *k*. The letter *k* has its usual sound, as in *kite* or *key.* The special spelling tells you that *ache* begins with the sound for ā and ends with the sound for *k*.

The special spelling also tells you which syllable to stress if a word has more than one syllable. Say the word *ruin* to yourself and listen to which syllable you say with more stress. The first syllable has more stress. Now do the same with the word *avoid.* The second syllable is said with more stress.

Look again at these words as they might appear, without their meanings, in a dictionary:

ru•in (rōō′ĭn)
a•void (ə void′)

The mark after the first part of the special spelling for *ruin* is called a **stress mark.** It shows that the part before it is said with more stress.

Use the special spelling and the pronunciation key to get the pronunciation for the following words.

fe•ro•cious (fə rō′ shəs)
guar•an•tee (găr′ ən tē)

Using a Pronunciation Key

One word in each of the following sentences is in boldface type. Read each sentence and look up those words in the Glossary. Use what you have learned to be sure that you have the correct meaning and pronunciation for each one. Be sure to stress the correct syllable as you say each word to yourself.

1. Kee's parents gave him a **mosaic** tile set.
2. The **rhythmic** sound of the rain put us to sleep.
3. Jodi is reading a story about a hideous **ogre**.
4. The **arena** was decorated for the show.
5. In size, Asia is **unique** because it is the largest continent in the world.

Skill Summary

- Special spellings show how to pronounce entry words in a dictionary.
- A pronunciation key tells you what the letters and marks in a special spelling mean.
- A word that has more than one syllable has a stress mark in the special spelling to show which syllable has the greater stress.

The Clue on the Porch

by Karen MacLeod

Clara and Miss Garcia are good friends. When something mysterious happens to her friend, Clara remembers a clue that solves the mystery. See if you can figure out the clue.

It was Tuesday, the day of Clara's dance class, and she was late. More than anything in the world, Clara wanted to be a ballerina, so she practiced hard. She was usually at Mrs. Trent's dance studio half an hour before her four o'clock class, warming up, and here it was past three-thirty, and Clara hadn't even left home yet.

"Bye, Mom," she called as she pulled on her coat. "I'm leaving for my dance class."

"Clara, wait," her mother said, appearing with a book in her hand. "Don't forget that you promised to drop this book off at Miss Garcia's house on your way to class."

"But, Mom, I'm late. Can't I take it tomorrow?" protested Clara.

"That's up to you, dear, but you did tell her that you would bring it to her today," said her mother.

Clara started for the door and then paused for a second. Miss Garcia lived only a block past the dance studio, so it wouldn't be too far out of her way. After all, she had made a promise. She took the book from her mother and flew out of the house.

As Clara jogged down the street, she thought about meeting Miss Garcia for the first time. Last summer a woman had passed by Clara's house with her dog strutting beside her. The dog was carrying the woman's handbag in its mouth. When Clara laughed at the sight, the woman explained that Max, her German shepherd, always carried her handbag when her arms were full of bundles.

After that Clara and Miss Garcia became good friends. Clara told Miss Garcia about her dream of dancing in a famous ballet company, and how she never missed a single dance class. One week last February, she had trudged through a terrible rainstorm to get to the dance studio. She was the only one who showed up for the class, and it turned out to be one of the best days of her life.

Miss Garcia told Clara how lonely she was when her sister Luisa first moved to Florida. But even though Luisa lives over two thousand miles away, they still are able to have lunch together every Tuesday. That's because every Sunday Miss Garcia and her sister both write long letters to each other. Then every Tuesday morning when the letters arrive, the two sisters sit down exactly at noon, have lunch, and read each other's letters.

Clara smiled to herself. "They're probably the only people in the world who have lunch together by mail," she thought.

It was five to four when Clara climbed the three steps to Miss Garcia's porch and rang the bell. She could hear Max barking in the back yard. Clara waited, but the door remained shut. Impatiently she rang again, but there was still no answer. She just couldn't wait any longer, so she placed the book at the foot of the door and left for her class.

The other dancers were already lining up at the barre when Clara arrived. She quickly found a place in line to begin the familiar exercises.

"Ready. *Plié,* one-two-three-four," Mrs. Trent's voice began. "Bend. Down. Up. Arm out. Again-two-three-four."

Clara's body moved automatically to the count, but her mind wandered back to Miss Garcia's front porch. Something there was not quite right. Some little thing nagged at Clara like a tiny stone in her shoe.

69

70

She pictured the door, a white lace curtain covering the glass front. Next to that was the mailbox with its lid slightly propped open by the edge of an envelope. Below were some of Miss Garcia's favorite plants. The two brown wicker chairs sat in the middle of the floor as usual. All normal. But something . . .

"Clara, are you with us?" Mrs. Trent's voice suddenly broke into her thoughts.

"Yes, Ma'am. I'm sorry." Clara, who always paid attention in class, suddenly realized that she was still facing the wall while the rest of the class had turned the other way. Embarrassed, she turned and continued the exercise.

Another thought popped into her mind. Miss Garcia must be home because she usually took Max wherever she went, even to her art class on Fridays. "Maybe she was next door," Clara reasoned. "After all, I was late, and Miss Garcia probably thought I forgot about bringing the book."

"Clara!" Mrs. Trent's voice exploded into her thoughts. "What is the matter today?"

"I'm sorry, Mrs. Trent." Clara looked around and saw that she was standing at the barre all alone. She walked to the center floor, putting Miss Garcia out of her mind, but the image of the porch reappeared.

"Of course," she said out loud.

Ignoring the puzzled looks of her teacher and classmates, Clara grabbed her coat and headed for the door. Without another word she was gone.

Clara ran all the way to Miss Garcia's house. She was sure that her friend was in trouble.

When she arrived at the house, everything was just as she had left it. She rang the doorbell and then rapped loudly on the glass. It was no use. Miss Garcia wouldn't — or maybe couldn't — answer. Clara would have to get into the house by herself. She tried the front door; it was locked.

Max had started barking in the back yard again. Maybe the back door was open! Clara walked down the driveway and scrambled over the fence. She was greeted by Max, who tugged at her sleeve with excitement, pulling her toward the door.

Sure enough, it was unlocked. As Clara opened the door, Max shot in ahead of her and disappeared.

"Miss Garcia," Clara called, "are you here?"

An instant later, Max came thumping up the basement stairs. "Max, where's Miss Garcia?" cried Clara.

The great dog barked once and then bounded back to the stairway. Clara followed him and switched on the basement light.

Lying at the bottom of the stairs, one leg twisted beneath her, was her friend Miss Garcia. Clara rushed down the stairs and took her hand. "Miss Garcia, Miss Garcia, wake up."

Miss Garcia opened her eyes slowly just for a moment and closed them again. Max settled down next to his owner, nuzzled his nose against her, and then whined softly.

The next few minutes became a hazy blur of sirens, flashing lights, and white-jacketed people taking Miss Garcia away on a stretcher. Then, as quickly as it had come, the ambulance was gone, leaving Clara and Max alone on the front porch. Clara hugged the big dog to her. "She'll be all right, Max," she whispered into his fur. "She'll have to be all right."

The next day dragged. Clara and her mother had arranged to visit Miss Garcia after school, and even

Clara's favorite classes seemed to go on for hours. Finally the three o'clock bell rang, and Clara ran out of the building and jumped into her mother's car.

At the hospital, they followed a nurse down a long hallway to Miss Garcia's room. Clara was relieved to see that the woman in the bed looked nothing like the crumpled heap she had seen lying at the bottom of the stairs the afternoon before. Although Miss Garcia was still a little weak and hampered by a cast on her leg, she was sitting up against her pillows and smiled as Clara and her mother walked into the room.

"I'm afraid I made you miss part of your ballet class yesterday," she said. Clara was about to say that it didn't matter as long as Miss Garcia was all right, but she just smiled. Her friend already knew how she felt.

"How are you?" Clara asked.

"Not bad, thank you — apart from having a heavy foot. The doctor tells me I was pretty lucky." Miss Garcia paused and then added, "And I was, in more ways than one. I fell down those stairs early in the morning, and I might have been there for days if you hadn't come along. I've been puzzling all day over how you knew I was in trouble. Was it Max?"

"Not really, Miss Garcia," Clara explained. "You see, there was a clue on your porch that finally tipped me off."

"A clue on my porch?" Miss Garcia echoed, looking even more puzzled. "What was it?"

Can you figure out what the clue on the porch was? Think about it carefully. Then turn the page upside-down and see if you're right.

Clue: The letter in the mailbox is the clue that tripped Clara off. Remember that Miss Garcia's sister's letter arrives every Tuesday and that she reads it at lunchtime. It was well past noon when Clara dropped off the book and saw the letter. It had not been taken out of the mailbox, so she knew that something must be wrong.

Author

Karen MacLeod says she gets her ideas for stories by watching people, by talking to them, and by reading — everything she can get her hands on. This story idea came from a newspaper item about a paper boy who saved a customer's life. Mrs. MacLeod has been a teacher and has written for magazines.

Thinking It Over

Comprehension Questions

1. What clue did Clara see on the porch that told her Miss Garcia was in trouble? Explain why this was a good clue.
2. Why did Clara have trouble paying attention in her dance class?
3. Who do you think called the ambulance? What makes you think that?
4. Do you think Max was a big help in leading Clara to Miss Garcia? Why?

Vocabulary

The words below name some ways people or animals move. Use each of the words in a sentence. You may use a different form of the word.

jog	**trudge**	**bound**
strut	**thump**	**scramble**

Writing a Letter

Pretend that you are Miss Garcia. Write a letter to your sister in Florida telling her about your accident and how you were found.

Thinking

by Felice Holman

Silently
Inside my head
Behind my eyes
A thought begins to grow and be
A part of me.
And then I think
I always knew
The thing I only got to know,
As though it always
Was right there
Inside my head
Behind my eyes
Where I keep things.

Words in Our Hands

by Ada Litchfield

Michael's parents are deaf — they
can't hear him when he talks.
But Michael and his parents have some
special ways to communicate.
Find out what they are.

name is Michael Turner, and I'm eight years
ave two sisters, Gina and Diane, a dog named
nd two parents who can't hear me when I talk.
've never heard me. You see, my mom and
born deaf. When they were babies, they
hear any sounds at all.

people think a person who can't hear can't
lk, but that's not true. My mom and dad
school for deaf children when they were
. That's where they learned to talk. They
placing their fingers on their teacher's
eeling how words *felt* in her voice box as
m. They learned how words *looked* by
face, especially her lips, as she spoke.
o learn to say words that way, but my
p

talk much now, but they are able to
ta's voice is high, and my dad's voice is
lounts have never heard other people's
voitheir own voices, so they don't know
howd. It's not always easy to understand
whaying, but Gina and Diane and I can
und.

S mother and father can understand
whataying by reading their lips. That's
anoth parents learned at their school —
lip rea

Rea difficult because some people don't
move their lips much when they talk, or they hide
their mouths with their hands. Besides, many words

look alike when you say them. Look in the mirror and say *pin* and *bin, hand* and *and, hill* and *ill.* See what I mean?

How we move our bodies and what our faces look like when we talk help our parents read our lips. Most of the time, however, we talk to them with our

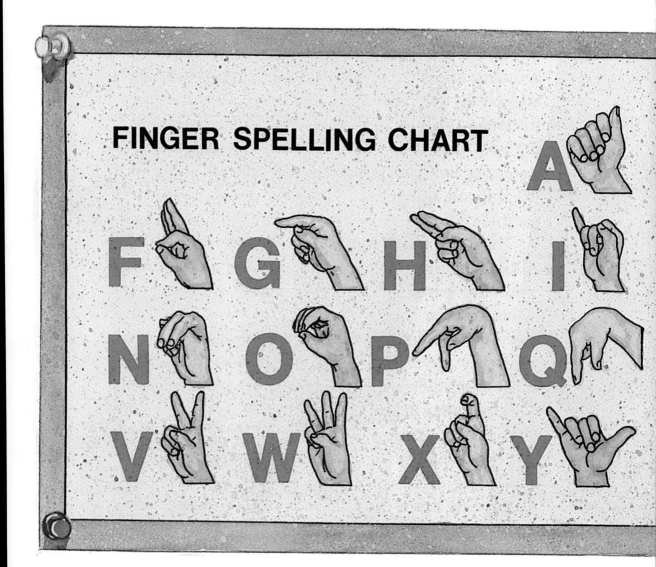

hands as well as our mouths. Grandma says we have words in our hands.

One way to talk with your hands is to learn a special alphabet so you can spell words with your fingers. This is called *finger spelling*.

Can you finger spell your name?

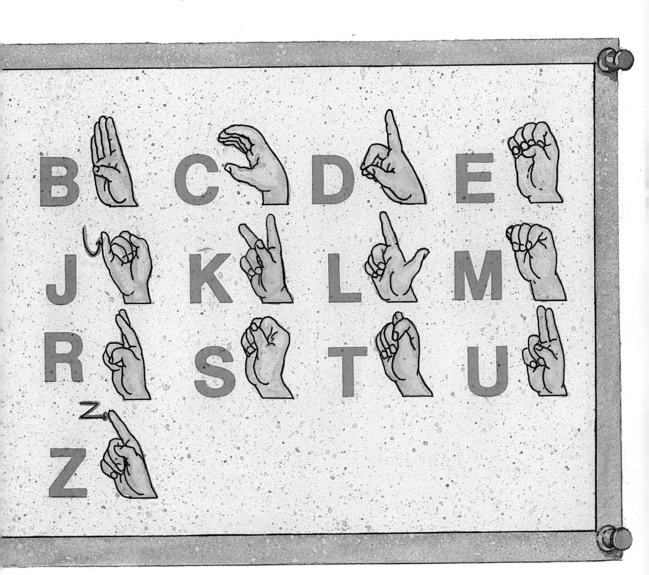

Another way to handtalk is to use sign language. You have to learn many signs that other people understand before you can talk in sign language. But once you have learned it, sign language is easier and faster than finger spelling.

Gina, Diane, and I are learning new signs all the time. My mom and dad learned sign language when they were little. They taught us signs when we were young, just as hearing parents teach their children words. Our grandparents, friends, and neighbors helped us learn to talk.

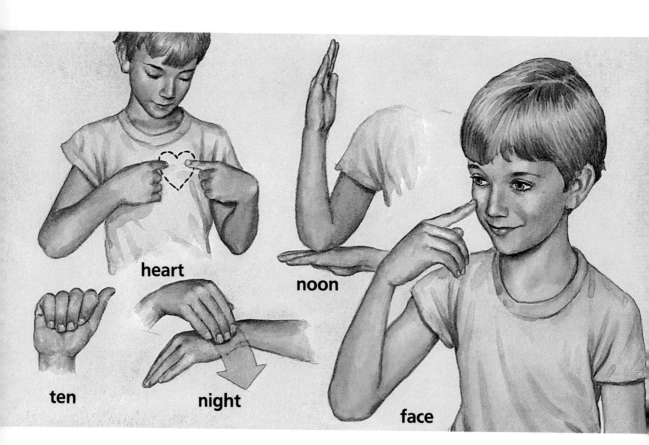

heart

noon

ten

night

face

There are five ways that Diane can ask my mother for a peanut butter sandwich.

She can make her mouth move slowly so my mother can read her lips.

She can finger spell *peanut butter* like this.

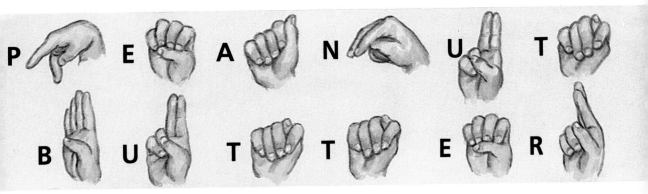

She can ask in sign language, which is easier than finger spelling.

peanut   butter   sandwich

She can print *peanut butter sandwich* on the writing pad my mom always carries with her.

Or she can lead my mother to the jar of peanut butter and point to it.

My parents have some special things to help them. In our house, when the telephone or doorbell rings, lights flash on and off. We also have a TTY attached to our phone. A TTY is a teletypewriter that spells out messages on paper or on a TV-like screen. Then my parents can type messages back.

Of course, the person calling us has to have a teletypewriter, and not very many hearing people do. That means that many times we kids have to talk on the phone for our parents. And sometimes we have to talk to people who come to the door.

When we were babies, my mom or dad checked on us frequently to be sure we were all right. They took turns at night. They used a cry alarm, which is a microphone that is hooked up to a light. When we cried, a light would flash in our parents' bedroom or in the kitchen or living room.

When Diane was little, Gina and I helped take care of her. We would hear when she cried and tell my mom or dad.

Some deaf people have hearing ear dogs to help them. We have Polly. Polly hasn't had lessons in hand signals the way real hearing ear dogs have, but she can do many things a hearing ear dog does.

She gets my mom up by tugging at her blankets if the flashing-light alarm doesn't wake her.

Polly runs back and forth to let my mom and dad know someone is at the door. She makes a big fuss if a flashing-light alarm goes off or if a pan is boiling over on the stove.

When Diane was a baby, Polly helped take care of her. Polly still follows Diane around and runs to tell my mom or dad if Diane gets into trouble.

Just because my parents are deaf doesn't mean we don't do things other families do. My mom and dad go to programs at school. We go on picnics. We have friends over for dinner and to stay all night. We drive to the city to the Science Museum.

It isn't true that a deaf person can't drive a car. Both my parents drive. They just have to depend on their eyes to avoid accidents. That's why we have rearview mirrors on both sides of our car.

We are a happy family. At least we were until about six months ago. Then the publishing company where my father has always worked moved to a new town, one hundred miles away.

My father is the editor of a magazine about farming, and he loves his job. Nobody in the family wanted to move, but we knew Dad wanted to go with his company.

We bought a new house with a big yard that everybody liked, but it took a long time to get used to our new town. Before, my mom had always done all the shopping and banking for our family. Now she felt a little uncomfortable going into a store or bank where the clerks didn't know her. Sometimes she wanted Gina or me to go with her.

In our old town, everybody knew our family. Nobody stared when they saw us talking with our hands, but in the new town, people did stare. Of course, they pretended they didn't see us, but I knew they were looking. Sometimes Gina and I felt embarrassed, and we didn't want to feel that way. We knew how shy my parents felt. We knew mom missed her art classes. We knew they both missed their old friends. We knew they were as lonesome and homesick as we were.

One day Gina's favorite teacher gave her a note to take home. It was an invitation for our family to go to a performance of the National Theatre of the Deaf.

At first, I didn't want to give the invitation to my parents. I didn't want them to go. I didn't want

people to stare at them or feel sorry for Gina and me.

Gina said they should go. She said that the play would be in sign language, and who would understand it better than our parents? I knew she was right. Besides, Mom and Dad needed to go out and meet new people.

Still, I was worried about what might happen. The night of the play, all sorts of questions were popping into my mind as I dragged up the steps into the auditorium.

The big hall was filled with people. Just inside the door, my mother signed to me, "Where will we sit?"

To our surprise, a man stood up and said, "There are five seats over here."

We couldn't believe it. He was talking to us in sign language!

All around us, people were laughing and talking. Many of them were talking with their hands.

Before the play started, we learned from our program that some of the actors were deaf and some could hear. The hearing actors and some of the deaf actors would speak in the play. All of the actors would sign, sometimes for themselves and sometimes for each other. Sometimes they would all sign together. Everyone in the audience would be able to understand what was going on.

The play we saw was called *The Wooden Boy*. It was about Pinocchio, a puppet who wanted to be a real boy. It was both funny and sad.

After the play, we went backstage to meet the actors. The deaf performers talked with people who knew sign language. The hearing actors helped the other people understand what was being said.

I was proud of my parents. They were smiling, and their fingers were flying as fast as anyone's. For the first time in many months, they seemed to feel at home.

Then we had another surprise. Gina's teacher came over to my mom. She talked very slowly and carefully so my mother could read her lips. Then she signed with her hands!

Gina was excited. Her favorite teacher, who wasn't deaf, had words in her hands too. Gina was learning something she didn't know before. We all were. We were learning there were many friendly

people in our new town who could talk with our parents. I decided this place wasn't going to be so bad after all.

I think some of the hearing people around us were learning something too. Maybe they never thought about it before, but being deaf doesn't mean you can't hear or talk. You can hear with your eyes and talk with your hands.

I'm glad that Gina and Diane and I know so many signs already. Why don't you learn a few yourself?

Author

While writing scripts for a TV series, Ada Litchfield found there were not many books for children about hearing problems, so she decided to write *A Button in Her Ear*, about a girl with a hearing aid, and *Words in Our Hands*, which you have just read. Mrs. Litchfield has written several other books about people with disabilities.

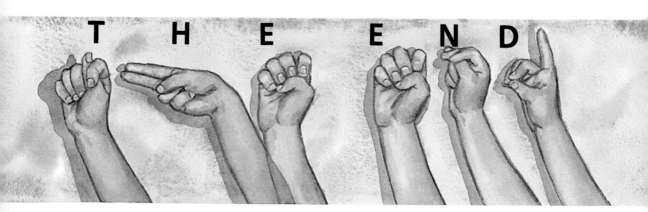

THE END

Thinking It Over

Comprehension Questions

1. What are some ways in which Michael and his parents communicate?
2. Where did Michael's parents learn to talk? How did they learn to talk?
3. How does Polly help Michael's parents?
4. Why did people in the new town stare at Michael and his family?
5. How did Michael's mother feel when the man answered her question in sign language? How did the whole family feel when they met the actors backstage?

Vocabulary

Use each word, or group of words, below in a sentence that tells something about the Turner family.

deaf	**alarm**	**message**
lip reading	**hearing ear**	**auditorium**

Writing About an Event

Pretend that you went to see the play with Michael and his family. Write about the play and about what happened backstage after the play.

THE NATIONAL THEATRE OF THE DEAF

Presents

THE WOODEN BOY

The pictures on these pages are from the play about Pinocchio, a wooden puppet who wants to be a real, live boy. Deaf and hearing actors perform in the play.

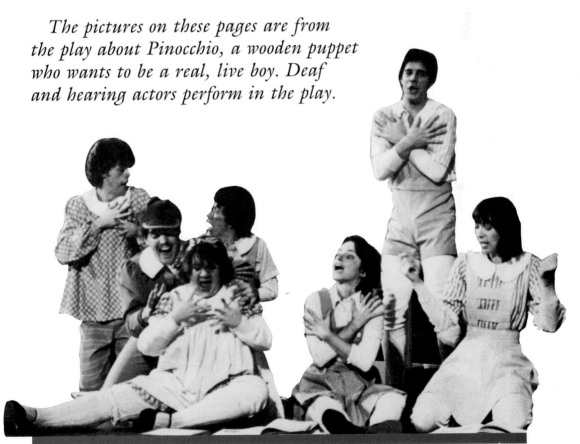

Brave Janet of Reachfar

by Jane Duncan

**Janet goes by herself to a dangerous place during
a wild snowstorm. Why does she go there?
Will she get back safely?**

Janet lived on a farm named Reachfar. It lay on top of a hill in the Highlands of Scotland and looked down toward the sea.

The nearest house to Reachfar was two miles away, but Janet never felt lonely. She had her dog, called Fly, and her family: her grandfather and grandmother, her father and mother, her aunt, and her special friends, Tom and George, who did most of the work about the farm.

Janet's grandfather was very old, with a long white beard, and he was a little deaf. Janet saw her father only in the evenings, for he managed another farm all day. Her grandfather, her grandmother, her mother, and Aunt Kate were always busy — especially her grandmother. Janet thought she must be the busiest woman in the whole world.

Granny was always bustling about and "laying down the law" or being "on about" things, as George and Tom called it. Only they did not call her Granny when she was on about things — they called her Herself.

One noonday in spring, when Janet and her family were sitting at the big kitchen table having their dinner, the sun suddenly seemed to disappear and the sky went dark. Big flakes of snow began to fly past the window.

"I *told* you this was coming," Granny said, and it was in her Herself voice.

Granny always seemed to know when it was going to rain and when there was going to be a gale.

"I said it was too early in the year to put the sheep out on the High Moor and the East Hill," Herself went on. "So don't blame me now that you have to go and bring them all back into the shelter of the Home Wood again."

She spoke as if everybody was arguing with her, but nobody was saying a word. Everybody was watching the snow, which kept growing thicker and thicker. "Finish your dinner, George and Tom, and fetch the sheep back into the Home Wood."

"Yes, Granny," Tom and George said together.

They put on their heavy coats and mufflers, took their tall sticks from the rack in the hall, and called their sheepdogs, Moss and Fan, out of the barn. They set off toward the gate that led to the High Moor. Janet followed them with Fly, but she did not go farther than the gate. The High Moor was a forbidden place.

"We will gather the big flock off the Heights first, Tom," George said at the gate. "Those thirty ewes on the East Hill will have to wait till we get back. Run along into the house, Janet, and get out of all this snow and cold."

Janet went into the stable to see Betsy, their horse. She climbed up to sit on the edge of Betsy's manger, while Fly lay down on a sack by the wall.

Stroking Betsy's face, Janet thought about her grandmother. She was rather beautiful, really. Her "on abouts" did not last for very long, and soon she would turn back into the person they called Granny, who was gentle and wise. She always seemed to know where you had been and what you had been up to, even when you were far away out of her sight. It seemed to Janet that Granny knew about every single thing in the whole world.

Janet gave Betsy's neck a final pat and climbed down from the manger.

She began to think of the poor sheep out on the cold East Hill. It would take George and Tom a long time to bring down the flock from the High Moor. The ewes on the East Hill would have a very long wait. . . .

Suddenly Janet buttoned up her coat and put on her woolen hood and gloves. "Heel, Fly," she said as they left the warm, steamy barn for the snow and cold out-of-doors.

The East Hill was a long way off, and today it seemed longer than ever. The wind kept trying to blow Janet and Fly backward as they plodded through the deepening snow on the path through the wood. At last, though, they came to the little gate that led out onto the bare hill where the snow was like a thick cloud of feathers.

When Janet took off her glove to undo the latch of the gate, her fingers went stiff with the cold. The East Hill was a forbidden place, too — but Janet did not intend to go right out on to it, not *right* out on to it.

"Seek, Fly!" she said, waving her arm at the hill, just like Tom or George. "Sheep! Go seek!"

The dog crouched low, so that her dark furry body seemed to slide under the blowing snow. She ran out onto the hill, while Janet waited in the shelter of the trees by the gate.

Soon the sheep began to come toward Janet. "One, two, three — " she counted as the woolly creatures galloped one by one through the narrow gateway, baa-ing as if to say thank you for the shelter of the trees.

"Twenty-nine," Janet said when Fly came to look up at her. "One more, Fly! Go seek!"

Fly disappeared into the snow again and was gone for a long time. When she came back, she brought no sheep with her. She put her paws up to Janet's chest and then began to dance round and round, barking all the time and making bigger and bigger circles that took her farther and farther out on the hill.

She wanted Janet to follow her, but Janet was not sure about this. Besides being forbidden, the East Hill under the blowing snow was very wild, bare, and frightening. In the end, though, she decided to trust Fly, who always knew the way home. She shut the little gate and stepped out into the deep snow and driving wind.

She was completely out of breath, and her legs felt as if they were going to break with tiredness when, at last, Fly nuzzled into a mound of snow and exposed the head of a sheep.

"Baa-aa," the sheep said in a weak, tired voice as Janet and Fly began to dig the snow away. Fly dug very quickly with her forepaws, making the snow fly up in a cloud behind her. But it was Janet who found the baby lamb, quite newly born and tucked in close to its mother.

"Stop, Fly," Janet said, for she knew that if she picked up the lamb and began to walk away, the mother sheep would struggle free and follow her.

Janet unbuttoned her coat, put the lamb inside, and fastened the coat again with the lamb's head sticking out between the two top buttons. When Janet and Fly started to walk away, the mother sheep began to struggle hard, baa-ing pitifully. It seemed she could not get up.

"Dig, Fly!" Janet said, and soon they found that a piece of the wire fence was wound round and round the sheep's leg. Her struggling was only pulling it tighter, so that it was cutting the leg painfully.

Janet's hands were not strong enough to bend the wire, though she tried for some time. At last she sat down in the snow. Fly sat down, too, her head on one side, her golden eyes looking from the sheep to Janet as if to say, "What do we do now?"

Janet thought hard. Then she took off her woolen hood and untied her blue hair ribbon. Her fingers were numb as she tied the ribbon tightly to Fly's collar. Her lips were stiff with cold, too, as she said, "George and Tom, Fly! George and Tom!"

With the wind behind her now, Fly dashed away, the ends of blue ribbon streaming from her collar.

Janet tucked herself close into the woolly side of the sheep, took off her wet gloves, and put her cold hands inside her coat to cuddle the lamb. She tried not to feel frightened.

The snow piled up around them, while the wind howled and shrieked across the hill. Janet began to feel warm, cozy, and sleepy. She did not know that this deceiving warm sleepiness sometimes causes people to snuggle down and be found long afterwards, frozen to death.

She was quite startled when she heard barking close beside her. Fly began to dig, her blue ribbon still streaming in the wind, and then Moss and Fan were there and began to dig too.

"Out of it! Get back, dogs!" said George's voice, and Janet found herself being lifted, shivering now, out of the snowy hole that had been so cozy and warm.

George turned her over his arm and began to pat her quite hard on the back. The shivering stopped.

"Careful!" she said, coming wide awake. "Mind my lamb, you clumsy big lump!"

"Why, she has a lamb!" Tom said.

"The mother sheep is hurt," Janet told them. "She has got wire ——"

"We'll soon see to that," Tom said, and with his strong fingers he began to untwist the wire that Janet had not been able to bend.

Janet was safe now from the storm, standing beside George and Tom, who always made everything safe. But she began to feel another kind of fear. She suddenly remembered that she was forbidden to come out onto the East Hill like this, and that there would be a scolding from Herself when she got home.

The mother sheep gave a loud "Baa!" and sprang to her feet. She was limping a little, but she would soon be all right. She came close to Janet to sniff at her lamb's head.

Janet looked up at George. "Herself and Mother are going to be angry," she said.

"Angry? After you bringing in the flock from the Hill and bringing home the first lamb of the spring?" George asked.

"About the East Hill, here," Janet said.

"*What* East Hill?" George asked, looking around as if he had never heard of the East Hill. "Speaking for myself, I cannot see anything through all this snow. I do not see any East Hill around here."

"Nor me either," Tom said. "And I will tell you something. We are going to be late for tea. Herself will be so angry about that, she'll have no angriness left for anything else. Come on!"

When they reached home, Herself looked from Tom to George, and then on to Janet with the lamb's head under her chin. This was her suspecting look — the look she wore when she suspected that Janet, George, and Tom had been up to something.

"Baa!" the little lamb said in a small voice.

"George and Tom," Herself said sternly, "take that lamb out to the fold to its mother where it belongs."

"Right away, Granny," George said.

"This very minute, Granny," Tom said.

"And you take those wet things off," she said to Janet, "and sit down at the table beside *your* mother where *you* belong."

Janet did as she was told, and Herself went on, "Sometimes I think the people of Reachfar have no sense at all, putting sheep out, taking them in, and prowling about among the snow and the cold as if they had no brains in their heads. It is a wonder that some of *them* don't get lost in the snow."

Janet's mother was very quiet and spoke always in a soft voice. "If they got lost in the snow, Granny, you would have nobody to scold. That would be terrible, wouldn't it?" she said.

Herself looked at Mother, and Janet watched her change back into Granny. Mother could always make her do this.

Granny smiled at Janet. "But you are a clever girl, finding the first lamb of the spring like that," she said. "Eat a big tea. You must be very hungry after going such a long, *long* way, all by yourself, to find that lamb."

Granny took the lid off the big black pot on the fire and stirred the supper soup. She had a funny smile on her face — a wise sort of smile that said she knew you had gone to a forbidden place but you had done it for a good reason and must be forgiven.

Janet ate a boiled egg, two scones with butter, and a piece of shortbread. It was a very nice tea.

Author

Jane Duncan, a Scottish author of many books for adults and children, had a family home in the far northern highlands of Scotland. It is the setting for the story you have just read. Janet's adventures continue in *Janet Reachfar and the Kelpie* and *Janet Reachfar and the Chickabird*, which were written just before the author's death in 1976.

Thinking It Over

Comprehension Questions

1. Why did Janet go to the East Hill during the snow-storm? Did she get back safely?
2. Fly led Janet to a mound of snow. What did Janet find under it?

108

3. When Janet sent Fly to get George and Tom, what did she do to let them know it was she who needed help?
4. Do you think Granny really knew that Janet had been on the East Hill? What makes you think that?

Vocabulary

Use the words in the box in sentences that tell about the story. You may use a different form of the word.

forbidden
wild
frightening
numb
howl
shriek
cozy
shiver

Writing a News Story

Pretend that Janet's adventure on the East Hill will be part of a local news broadcast. Write the story. In your news story, try to answer the questions *who, what, when, where, why,* and *how.*

Prefixes and Suffixes

There are words that can be made into new words by adding parts to them. When you add a new part to a word, you may change the meaning.

One kind of word part is called a **prefix**. A prefix may be added at the beginning of a base word. The prefix *un-* means "not." Add *un-* to the word *real* and you will get *un-real*, which means "not real."

Another kind of word part is called a **suffix**. A suffix may be added to the end of a base word. The suffix *-ly* means "in a certain way." Add *-ly* to the word *slow* and you will get *slowly*, which means "in a slow way."

110

Knowing the meanings of prefixes and suffixes can help you figure out what new words mean. Below are some new words that have been made by adding *un-* and *-ly* to the word *kind.*

unkind means "not kind"
kindly means "in a kind way"
unkindly means "not in a kind way"

On a piece of paper make two columns. Number them 1 to 4. Then make some new words by adding *un-* and *-ly* to the words on this page.

un-
1. ____safe
2. ____wrapped
3. ____clear
4. ____usual

-ly
1. loud____
2. helpful____
3. close____
4. proud____

Now copy the sentences below. In the sentences, use the new words you have made.

1. Pam and I cheered _____ when we _____ the box.

2. The directions to our Magic Castle Kit seemed _____, even though we studied the plan _____ .

3. Sharp glass can be _____, so Dad _____ put in the castle's windows.

4. After our _____ castle was finished, we _____ showed it to the family.

"Warton's Dilemma"

an excerpt from
A Toad for Tuesday

written by
Russell E. Erickson

illustrated by
Doug Cushman

This is the first of a series of books about two toad brothers. In the series the author makes you laugh even though you worry about Warton, the toad, and the strange and unexpected things that happen to him and to his brother, Morton.

In this excerpt, a terrible owl and Warton become involved in a thrilling adventure. This unusual story includes exciting action as well as lively and interesting conversation between the toad and the owl.

A TOAD FOR TUESDAY

written by Russell E. Erickson

illustrated by Doug Cushman

Warton's Dilemma

In the middle of winter, Warton the toad decided to take some delicious beetle brittle to his Aunt Toolia. His brother, Morton, tried to talk him out of it, but Warton's mind was set. He put on his heaviest sweaters and strapped on his homemade skis. His brother packed some food for him and wished him luck.

On the way, Warton rescued a mouse that was half-buried in the snow. The grateful mouse gave Warton a bright red scarf. If Warton wore the scarf, the mouse said, all of the mouse's relatives would know that the toad was a friend, and they would help him if he ever got into trouble. The mouse also warned Warton about a dangerous owl who hunted

114

by day, when other owls slept. No sooner had Warton left the mouse than he found himself being chased by this owl. In trying to escape, Warton crashed into a pile of stones, hurting his foot and losing his skis. Suddenly, he was grabbed by strong claws and lifted into the air. The owl carried Warton to his home — a hole near the top of an oak tree. Warton looked around. . . .

It was dark inside and smelled musty. The owl sat him in a corner and stepped back. He gave the toad a piercing look.

"What's your name?" he said.

"Warton."

"Warton?" said the owl. "Well, I think I'll call you — Warty."

"I don't care for that very much."

"You don't? Well, that's too bad . . . Warty!"

The little toad got up all his courage and looked right at the owl. "Are . . . are you going to eat me?"

The owl opened his yellow eyes wide. "Am I going to eat you? Of course I'm going to eat you!" Then the owl walked across the room. On the wall a large calendar hung crookedly. The owl pointed to it. "Do you know what this says?"

The toad looked at it closely. "Yes, it says BERNIE'S GARAGE — BRAKES AND FRONT ENDS OUR SPECIALTY."

"No! I don't mean that. You're not very bright, are you? It says that in five days it will be Tuesday, and next Tuesday happens to be my birthday. And finding a little toad in the middle of winter is going to make me a special birthday treat. So, until that day, Warty, you may do as you please. From the looks of your foot, I needn't worry about your trying to hop away. Besides, there is no way you can possibly get down from this tree."

The toad looked at his foot. It was twice its normal size. He gave a big sigh, and then he glanced around. . . .

"As long as I am here, I would like to make myself comfortable," said Warton. "Do you mind if I light some candles? It seems very dreary in here."

"Dreary?" said the owl. "It seems dreary? Well, go ahead if you want to. It doesn't matter to me."

The toad dug into his pack and pulled out two beeswax candles. As soon as they were lit and began casting their warm glow about the room, he felt much better. He began to straighten his

corner. And, being of a cheerful nature, he began to hum a little tune.

The owl couldn't believe his ears. "Warty, you did hear me say that I was going to eat you next Tuesday, didn't you?"

"Yes," said the toad.

The owl shook his head.

Warton continued to busy himself in his corner. Then he turned to the owl and said, "What's your name?"

"I don't know," said the owl. "I guess I don't have one."

"What do your friends call you?"

"I don't have any friends."

"That's too bad," said Warton.

"No, it isn't too bad," snapped the owl, "because I don't want any friends and I don't need any friends. Now, be quiet!"

Warton nodded. After a while he said, "If you did have a name, what would you like it to be?"

The owl began to be a little flustered. He wasn't used to talking to anyone, especially in his home. "Well, if I had a name . . ." he said slowly, "if I had a name . . . if I had a name, . . . I think I would like . . . George."

"Uh-huh," said the toad. He went back to straightening his corner.

The owl was becoming sleepy. He fluffed his feathers and closed his eyes.

Just as he was beginning to doze off, the toad called, "Hey, George!"

The owl's eyes popped open. "Are you talking to me?"

"Yes," said the toad. "Do you mind if I make some tea?"

"Oh, go ahead," said the flabbergasted owl.

Warton took some more things out of his pack and prepared the tea. . . . Shortly, he had a steaming pot of refreshing tea.

"It's ready, George," said the toad.

"What's ready?" growled the sleepy owl.

"Our tea," replied the toad.

"I don't want any."

"But I've already got it poured," said Warton.

"Oh, all right," grumbled the owl.

So, by the light of the beeswax candles, the owl and the toad sat down to tea. . . .

Then the toad talked, and the owl listened. Then the owl talked, and the toad listened. It wasn't until the latest hours of the night that the owl finally said, "I'm too tired to talk anymore." And he went to sleep.

Warton put away the teacups, and then he put out the beeswax candles. As he lay in the still darkness, he tried very hard to think of what he should do. But, because of the very busy day he had had and because of all the new experiences, his tired head just would not work at all. He was soon snoring softly.

When the toad awoke the next morning, the owl was gone. The swelling on Warton's foot had gone down, but it was still quite sore. . . .

Warton poked through his pack trying to find something that would be just right for breakfast. He selected an ant-egg salad sandwich. As he unwrapped it, his eyes turned to the wall opposite the doorway. A ray of sunlight fell directly on

120

the owl's calendar. A large circle had been drawn around the day of his birthday, and an X put upon the day just past.

Only five days were left!

Warton's appetite nearly vanished, but he managed to eat his breakfast. When he was finished, he went to the doorway and looked out.

The snow-covered ground was far, far below, and there was not a branch anywhere near that he could jump to. And even if he did somehow get down from the tree, his foot was still too sore to travel on. "I shall just have to wait a bit," he thought.

All this time, Warton had been studying the owl's home. Now something was bothering him as much as the coming of next Tuesday. That was the sorry state of the owl's housekeeping.

Warton could stand it no longer. Immediately he set about cleaning up the mess. . . .

All morning and all afternoon he cleaned. He didn't even stop for lunch. He had barely finished his work when he heard the soft flapping of wings.

The owl had returned a little earlier than usual. He had never thought of cleaning his home, so he was astonished at what he saw.

"It doesn't look too bad, Warty," he said. Then he puffed himself up, and his eyes opened wide. "But don't think I'm going to change my mind about next Tuesday."

"I didn't do it for that reason," said Warton. He went to his pack, . . . unwrapped another of the sandwiches Morton had made for him, and quietly ate his supper. . . .

When Warton swallowed the very last bite, the owl said, "Are you going to make tea again tonight?"

"Perhaps I will," said Warton.

"Perhaps I will have some, too," said the owl softly.

So that night the toad and the owl once again sat down to tea. And once again it was very late before they went to sleep.

122

A Plan of Escape

The following morning, when the toad awoke, the owl was gone as before. Warton's foot felt much better, so the first thing he did was to look at the calendar. "Only four more days — I must do something soon," he thought anxiously.

He went to the doorway and looked down — it was still just as far to the bottom of the tree. . . .

He decided to clean the owl's home again. When there was nothing left to clean, he ate his lunch. Then he did some jumping exercises to clear his head for serious thinking. When his head was clear, he squatted under the kitchen table and began to think.

First one eye blinked, then the other. Slowly, at first, then faster and faster he blinked, until everything became a blur. Then he stopped, smiling.

He hopped to the doorway again and looked down. "I think two and a half will do it," he said, hopping back to his corner. Opening his pack, he took out his three tightly-knitted sweaters — the blue one, the yellow one, and the white one with the red reindeer.

"There is more than enough strong yarn here to reach the bottom of this tree," he thought.

He began unraveling the blue sweater. And as he unraveled, he tied small loops in the yarn, just far enough apart for him to step into.

"This ladder is going to take me a couple of days," he thought, looking anxiously at the calendar. . . .

For the rest of the day, he unraveled and made loops and hummed softly. When he thought it was almost time for the owl to come home, he hid everything in his pack.

It was none too soon, for the owl returned even earlier than he had the day before. After supper the two had tea. . . .

As the toad filled their cups again, the owl said, "This is very good tea."

"Yes, it is," said Warton, "but not as good as my favorite of all teas."

"What is that?" asked the owl.

"Juniper-berry tea. My cousin once brought me some. I've never tasted any as good. But it grows only in certain places, and I've never had it again."

And they talked some more.

After Warton blew out the beeswax candles, he said, "Goodnight, George."

There was a long silence. Then the owl said, "Goodnight, Warty."

The next day was just the same. In the morning when the toad awoke, the owl was gone. Warton worked on his unraveled-sweater-ladder until the owl returned. Later, they drank some tea and had a chat.

On Sunday morning, even though his ladder wasn't finished, Warton decided to test it. He fastened one end to the owl's saggy sofa. The other end he dropped out of the doorway. Lying on his belly, he placed one foot over the edge and into the first loop. That one held. . . .

But Warton had to be sure that his ladder would really work. So down he went to another loop, another, and then another. Finally he was satisfied. Climbing back up was much, *much* more difficult.

Warton was all out of breath when he crawled into the owl's home. . . .

As he put the ladder in his pack, a thought came to him, "Maybe George will change his mind. Then I won't need this ladder at all." Warton was thinking about how the owl came home earlier and earlier each day and how he seemed to enjoy their chats very much. At times he even seemed almost friendly. "Why, he may not eat me after all!" The thought suddenly made Warton feel quite happy.

But that day, the owl returned home later than he had ever done before. It was almost dark when he stepped through the doorway.

Warton was still feeling quite happy. "Good evening, George," he said cheerily. "Did you have a nice day today?"

The owl stood staring down at the toad, his eyes cold as ice. "No . . ." he said slowly, "I did not have a nice day. . . ."

Warton's happiness vanished instantly. He knew now that to depend upon the owl's having a change of heart could be a fatal mistake. The ladder was his only hope, and yet there was so much more work to do and — the toad sighed — so little time. . . .

Then the worst thing happened: The owl discovered Warton's ladder and threw it away. He was very angry and wouldn't speak to the toad all evening. The next morning, on Warton's last day, the owl left as usual. Soon after, the toad heard a strange scratching sound that kept getting louder and louder. A hole suddenly appeared in the wall, and a mouse climbed into the room. He said his name was Sy. He had seen Warton's red scarf, and he and his family had decided to rescue the toad. Warton quickly packed and followed Sy through a tunnel that led outside. There he saw one hundred mice on skis. The mice had made them after seeing Warton ski. Forming two lines, Warton and the mice set out for Aunt Toolia's.

After a while, they stopped to rest in an open meadow, where something caught Warton's eye.

Down below, near the stream, some kind of a struggle was going on. Puffs of snow flew in every direction. Even from such a distance, a great deal of screeching and growling could be heard. When the snow cleared away for an instant, Warton saw someone he thought he knew.

"George?" he said under his breath. Shading his eyes from the bright sun, he looked again.

He was right. George the owl was struggling frantically to free himself from the jaws of a snarling fox. Warton could see at once that George didn't have the slimmest chance. Even now, the owl's wings were flapping weakly against the snow, while flying feathers filled the air.

Warton hopped to his feet and strapped on his skis.

"Where are you going?" asked Sy.

"I'm going to help George."

"George? Who's George?"

"George, the owl," said Warton.

"But . . . but . . . I thought we were helping you to get away from the owl," said Sy in bewilderment.

"Yes," said Warton, "but I just can't stand here and watch that fox eat him."

"But, he was going to eat *you*," protested Sy.

Warton wasn't listening. He pushed off toward the icy stream.

Sy scratched his head. "I never did understand toads. Well, come on, everyone!" he squeaked with a twitch of his whiskers. "Let's give him a hand."

At once, all the mice jumped onto their skis and pushed off after Warton. The sunny hillside was one great wave of skiing mice as they flashed over the glistening snow. A powdery cloud rose high behind them as the one hundred mice and one toad swept downward.

The fox looked up and blinked unbelievingly. Faster and faster they came, the sharp points of their poles glittering like diamonds and each one pointing straight at him. Quickly the fox decided that he wanted no part of whatever it was.

He released the owl and bounded off through the deep snow as fast as his shaking legs would go. . . .

Warton looked sideways at the crumpled owl. Feathers were scattered all over the snow. Some floated slowly away in the icy stream. The owl's

131

wings were badly tattered, and one of his big yellow eyes was swollen completely shut.

As he looked at the once proud bird, Warton felt sad.

"Hello, Warty," said the owl weakly.

"Hello, George," said the toad.

"What are you doing here?" asked the owl.

"I'm escaping."

The owl's one good eye opened wide. "Escaping? Escaping from what?" he said, clearly annoyed.

"From you," said the toad. "Today is your birthday, and you said you were going to eat me. I was to be your special treat."

The owl started to shake his head, but it hurt too much. "Didn't you see my note?" he said, sounding more and more exasperated.

"No, I — I was in such a hurry to leave."

"Well, if you had, you would have known that I was coming home soon, and that I was going to bring a surprise."

"A surprise?" said Warton.

"That's what I said. I first came here to the stream to get a nice fish for supper, which I did. But the surprise is over there, and that's where the fox caught me." The owl turned and pointed to some bluish-green bushes.

"Why, those are juniper bushes," said the toad.

"That's right," said the owl. "You said juniper berries made your favorite kind of tea, didn't you?"

Warton hardly knew what to say. "But I don't understand. . . . Do you mean you came here to pick them for me, and you weren't going to eat me, ever?"

"Of course I was going to eat you — until last night, that is." The owl spoke more softly. "Because we weren't speaking, I thought quite a bit last night. I thought about our chats and other things, and I thought that perhaps having a friend might not be too bad. I mean . . . I don't need any friends, of course, . . . but . . . if I ever do have a friend, . . . I hope he is just like you . . . Warton. . . ."

The toad hopped around to where he could look up at him. "I would be happy to be your friend, George."

The owl looked down, and a big smile slowly spread across his battered face. "Well, that's fine. That's just fine. I'm so happy I promise I'll never eat another toad again." He looked around at Sy and his family. "Or a mouse, for that matter."

The mice cheered.

"Now, if I can still fly," he said, shaking out a few more loose feathers, "I'd be glad to take you the rest of the way to your Aunt Toolia's."

The toad hopped onto his back, shouting good-by and thank you to Sy and to all his family. It took the owl some time to lift out of the snow,

but finally he rose into the air. The higher he flew, the stronger he became. Warton waved to the mice as, far below, they grew smaller and smaller. Then the forest trees seemed to float beneath them as they made a great circle in the blue sky and turned toward Aunt Toolia's.

Author

A Toad for Tuesday is the first book Russell Erickson wrote about the two toad brothers, Warton and Morton. This book was honored by the American Library Association as a Notable Children's Book, and it was chosen as an outstanding book by the Child Study Association. Mr. Erickson went on to write more adventures of the funny pair, including *Warton and Morton*, and *Warton and the Castaways*.

Illustrator

Doug Cushman, an artist from New Haven, Connecticut, is an illustrator of many children's books. The books he has illustrated include *Not Counting Monsters, Trolls, Giants* and *Once Upon a Pig*. His well-illustrated book *Bicycle Bear* was honored by the International Reading Association's book list *Children's Choices*.

Comprehension Questions

1. Did Warton and the owl finally become friends? How did this friendship save Warton and the owl?
2. What clues were there in the story that told you George was beginning to like Warton?
3. If you had been Warton, would you have tried to save George? Why?
4. What promise did George make at the end of the story? Find his exact words on page 134.

Vocabulary

The author used the words below to tell how the owl felt or looked at different times in the story. Use each word in a sentence that tells when in the story the owl felt or looked this way.

flustered   **annoyed**   **astonished**
flabbergasted   **exasperated**   **crumpled**

Writing a Diary Entry

Pretend that you are George the owl and that you keep a diary. Write in your diary why you changed your mind about eating Warton.

Magazine Wrap-up

Story Characters

Some of the characters from the stories in this magazine are listed below. These characters found something that made them happy. What did each character find? Tell who else was made happy in each story and how.

Owney
Johnny
Clara
Janet

Vocabulary

Look at the words below.

hoot	**shriek**
train	**trip**
frightening	**screech**
shift	**flabbergasted**
annoyed	**howl**

1. Which words have more than one meaning?
2. Which words express feelings?
3. Which words are "sound" words?

Pronunciation Key

Look up the boldface words below in the Glossary at the back of this book. Number a paper from 1 to 6. Beside each number write the key word for the vowel sound in each word. Then use each boldface word in a sentence.

shift	**fault**
fame	**heap**
scram	**crouch**

Writing About a Visit

The characters you read about in this magazine lived in different places and at different times. They also did many interesting things. Think about the characters, their homes, and their activities. Write about a character you would like to visit and tell why.

Books to Enjoy

Cornrows
by Camille Yarbrough
A girl and her brother hear marvelous stories about their black heritage from their mother and grandmother.

Cam Jansen and the Mystery of the Babe Ruth Baseball
by David A. Adler
Cam uses her special skills to catch the thief who stole a valuable baseball.

Pets Without Homes
by Caroline Arnold
This book tells how an animal shelter takes care of Max and Buffy, a lost cat and a lost dog.

Toad Food and Measle Soup
by Christine McDonnell
In five funny stories, Leo learns about vegetarian cooking and has other adventures at home and at school.

139

Journeys
Magazine Two

Contents

142

HARALD and the GIANT KNIGHT

by Donald Carrick

Harald thinks the baron's knights are wonderful. He longs to be one of them. Will he change his mind when he gets a chance to spend some time with them?

Harald lived with his mother, Helga, and his father, Walter, in the valley that spread beneath the castle. The valley was owned by a baron who lived in the castle, surrounded by his knights. All the farmers in the valley had to give the baron part of their crops. He, in turn, allowed them to farm his land. Harald's family had farmed the same land for as long as anyone could remember.

Harald's father was a weaver as well as a farmer. He wove screens, hats, fences, chairs, and every type of basket.

One spring morning, Harald climbed up to the castle with baskets his father had woven for the castle kitchen. Harald went to the castle as often as he could.

After he delivered the baskets, he wandered through the passageways, exploring the wondrous stone chambers. Many of the rooms were larger than his home.

Harald was especially fond of the baron's knights. Knights were different from other folk. They wore leather and metal clothes covered by bright tunics. The knights spoke with deep voices and their clothing creaked and clanked as they walked by. Harald longed to be one of them.

Harald loved the jousts when two knights practiced against one another. Best of all were the tournaments. Then he could watch all the baron's knights clash with all the knights from another castle in a

mock battle. Nothing made Harald happier than to see the galloping horses and the swirling banners.

On this particular morning, the baron announced that it was time to begin training for the summer tournaments. A great cheer went up from the knights. They were restless after the long winter they had spent inside the castle.

As Harald walked home, he wished he could train with them.

The next morning, a terrible racket woke Harald. He ran outside to find his father in a fit. Men from the castle were swarming all over their farm. Horns blew and kettledrums boomed. Tents were going up.

"What's happening?" Harald asked.

"The knights' regular practice fields are flooded, so they've come here to train," his father said.

Harald watched as knights strutted about, shouting a thousand orders.

"We are ruined," groaned Walter. "With all this foolish practice on our fields, how can we plant the spring crops?"

Harald understood how his father felt. Without a harvest, his family would have no food and could not pay the baron for the use of his land. But at the same time, it was Harald's dream come true. All the knights were right here on his family's farm!

Walter's fields were transformed into an arena in which the knights galloped about on large horses and practiced their jousting.

Since no farming could be done, Harald spent all his time at the knights' camp. Soon he was helping with the horses and tending the fires. Perhaps there was a chance for him to become a knight after all.

The knights' presence changed everything on the farm. There were no more eggs to collect because the constant noise caused the chickens to stop laying. The pigs grew nervous and lost weight.

The knights had huge appetites. Walter and the other valley farmers had to supply them with chickens, ducks, pigs, and goats for their stew pots and roasting spits.

Harald was upset and disappointed. He had always thought knights were strong, brave men who spent their time helping people. Instead, he saw them thoughtlessly ruining the fields and eating all the farmers' food.

Walter was pleased when Harald announced one day that he was no longer going to the camp. Harald had lost his taste for the knightly life.

To save what little food they had left, Helga gathered it together and put it in a sack. When it was dark, Harald went with his father to hide it. They carried the food down a small path past the knights' camp to a secret cave. Harald had discovered the cave one day while he was picking berries. They hid the food on a high ledge.

When they returned home, no one could sleep so they sat together around their small fire. There seemed to be no answer to their problem.

"If I were big, I'd force the knights to leave," said Harald.

"No one is big enough to do that," answered Helga, "except another knight."

Walter said nothing, but his hands began weaving. The giant shadows his father cast on the wall gave Harald an idea.

"I know how we can get rid of the knights!" he said.

His father stopped weaving. "What do you mean, son?" he asked.

"Well, why can't we make a knight to frighten them?"

"Just how would we do that, Harald?" asked Helga.

"Father is an expert weaver, isn't he? He can weave just about anything. Why can't he weave a giant knight?"

A smile spread over Walter's face. "Let's hear more," he said.

Excitedly they talked late into the night as idea led to idea. By morning, they had a plan.

From the next day on, Harald's family spent all their time at the cave weaving their giant. Harald made trip after trip to the cave, bringing Walter great bundles of reeds.

With each bundle of reeds, the basket knight grew larger. Harald was very proud of his father's skill. He was sure nothing this large had ever been woven.

"By daylight, he will probably look rather patchy," Walter said. "But by night, after the knights have finished eating and are asleep, our knight should be very frightening."

Helga decided to make a cape for him.

Finally the giant basket knight was finished. He was almost too large to squeeze through the cave entrance. Carefully they mounted the creature on Patience, their old plow horse, and tied it down.

Walter led Patience down the narrow trail. The knight looked huge but weighed so little that each draft from the valley caught it like a sail. Harald clung to a rope to steady the creature.

At one spot the trees were so close that they almost pushed the basket giant off Patience's back. When the knight swayed back and forth it looked even more ghost-like.

"These paths were not made for giants," Harald whispered.

Each small farm along the way had a dog that barked as the giant drew near. Harald started to shiver. What if they were discovered? Fortunately no one woke up.

When they arrived at the edge of camp, the knights were all asleep.

It was Harald's task to enter the camp and untie the horses. He slipped quietly past the tents full of snoring knights. By day he knew the camp, but by night it all seemed different. One mistake could ruin everything.

At last he found the horses and with trembling hands untied the knots. The freed horses began to wander through the camp.

In the light of the early moon, Harald saw the giant loom above the trees. The moment the giant knight appeared, Walter and Helga began a terrifying clamor. She clanged pots while he made loud, moaning sounds through a long wooden tube.

That was the signal for Harald to dart from tent to tent, pulling up tent pegs. One after another, the tents collapsed on the sleeping knights.

The bewildered knights awoke in the dark, blanketed by the heavy tents. As they groped free, they tripped over ropes and cracked their shins on tent poles.

Once they were in the open, the knights were startled by the sight of the giant, who seemed to be walking over the trees. It began to shout at them in a deep, creaky voice.

"AWAY WITH YOU! BEGONE, ALL OF YOU, BEFORE THE NEW DAY DAWNS!"

Then, suddenly, the swaying knight seemed to disappear from the sky. The frightened knights were left standing in the shambles of the camp. Actually,

the giant had fallen from Patience's back and she had trotted away, dragging him behind.

Harald caught up with his parents, who were close on Patience's heels. They were busy picking up the bits and pieces that were falling from the giant. There was no time to wonder if their plan had worked until they reached the cave.

Dumbfounded, the knights milled about the camp trying to gather their horses. No trace of the ghostly giant could be found.

No one wanted to mention the ghost's warning, but one knight had the courage to say, "This camp is a wreck. I think it's time to leave."

"Let's go back to the castle," said a second.

A great sigh of relief came from all sides. Not one knight wanted to stay on and risk seeing the giant again.

Shortly after sunrise, Harald, Helga, and Walter watched the band of knights make their way slowly up the hill toward the castle. Helga and Walter hugged each other and cried with relief. Harald, who could not contain himself, jumped for joy.

After a great deal of work, the three of them cleared their fields and planted crops. That fall their harvest was not as big as usual, but it was enough to pay the baron and feed themselves throughout the winter.

The next spring Harald and his father were planting once again.

"Listen to what the wind brings us from down the valley," said Walter.

They could hear a faint clanging from the knights at practice on the baron's field. This time they were but pleasant tinkles to Harald's ears.

Nearby stood a familiar figure. It was a scarecrow, fashioned from the giant's reeds. As it turned with the wind, it almost seemed to smile.

Author

The idea for this story came from Donald Carrick's two young sons. With their encouragement, he studied life in medieval Europe, castles, and peasant farms. Then he wrote and illustrated *Harald and the Giant Knight*.

Mr. Carrick has written and illustrated other books. One that you might enjoy reading is *Morgan and the Artist,* the story of a little painted figure that comes to life. Mr. Carrick has also illustrated over twenty books written by his wife, Carol.

Thinking It Over

Comprehension Questions

1. Why did Harald change his mind about wanting to be one of the baron's knights?
2. Why did the knights go to Walter's fields to train for the summer tournaments?
3. How were Harald and his parents able to save a little food for themselves?
4. Do you think the knights will train on Walter's, or another farmer's fields again? Why or why not?

Vocabulary

The words below can be used to describe the knights' feelings and actions at different times in the story. Use the words in sentences to tell when the knights felt or acted that way.

restless   bewildered

thoughtlessly   dumbfounded

frightened   startled

Writing a Conversation

Pretend that you are having a conversation with one of the knights. Write the conversation. In the conversation, have the knight explain what took place on the night the giant knight appeared.

Synonyms

How would you rate this dragon?

☐ **frightening**   ☐ **startling**   ☐ **terrifying**

Some things are alike in certain ways, and words can be similar too. They can have meanings that are nearly the same as other words. Such words are called **synonyms**. Authors often use synonyms so that they do not repeat the same words.

The words *startling*, *frightening*, and *terrifying* are synonyms because they have almost the same meaning. Each of these words can be used to describe something scary; however, each word is a little different in meaning. The sentences below show how the words are different.

1. The distant howl that the villagers heard during the night was **frightening**.
2. When the dragon finally appeared, its size was **startling.**
3. The dragon was enormous, with fierce eyes, fiery nostrils, and a hideous mouth. It was really **terrifying**.

162

Using words that mean "scary," but that are still a little different in meaning, makes the description in each sentence more accurate. Authors use synonyms in this way to make their stories interesting.

Number a paper from 1 to 4. Copy the sentences that follow. Choose a word from the list below each sentence to use in place of the blank. Try to choose a word that gives an accurate description.

1. This _____ castle has one thousand rooms.
   huge
   giant
   enormous

2. The view from the highest tower is _____ .
   wonderful
   astonishing
   magnificent

3. Even on _____ days the view is fairly good.
   gloomy
   dull
   dreary

4. From the top of the castle, the people below look

   _____ .
   tiny
   little
   small

Hannah Is a Palindrome

by Mindy Warshaw Skolsky

Hannah wants to be a teacher when she
grows up. She thinks that being class monitor
would be good practice — and fun too. Is

There were two things in school Hannah had never been picked to be. The first was monitor when the teacher had to leave the room. The second was the person who clapped erasers together to clean the chalk dust out. "I wonder if Miss Pepper knows about that," thought Hannah.

So one morning she wrote a note in school, and it said:

Dear Miss Pepper,
    Did you know that I was never monitor and also I never clapped erasers?
    I wish I could do one or two of those things, because I am going to be a teacher.
Best of all, I'd like to be a monitor.

                        Love,
                        Hannah

P.S. I also like to clap erasers.

Then she went up to the pencil sharpener and sharpened her pencil. On the way back to her seat, she dropped the note on Miss Pepper's desk.

Miss Pepper cleared her throat. She opened the drawer at the top of her desk and took out a little box. Hannah looked to see if it said "Cherry" or "Licorice." Miss Pepper always had a supply of cherry and licorice fruit drops in her desk. "I have a dry throat," she would say. Hannah loved cherry *and* licorice fruit drops. She could never decide which she liked better. When somebody was monitor, if the room remained quiet while Miss Pepper was gone, she would say, "Well done," when she got back. Then she would say to the monitor, "Would you like a cherry or a licorice fruit drop?"

Hannah dreamed of being a monitor and being offered cherry or licorice, but in her dream she could never decide which. Sometimes Hannah still had trouble making up her mind. But she didn't want Miss Pepper to know that, because Miss Pepper had a rule, "Don't be indecisive." Hannah had looked up *indecisive* in the dictionary, and she decided that rule meant "Make up your mind."

Miss Pepper stood up.

"It is time for our new word of the day," she said. "It's a big one."

Miss Pepper loved big words. She gave a new one every day. She always wrote the new word in a special place on the blackboard, and then she asked someone to look it up in the dictionary. That person had to tell the definition, and then everybody wrote it five times. Then they took it home for homework and wrote it five more times and made up a sentence with the new word in it.

All the children liked to be picked to be monitor or clap erasers; but nobody liked to be picked to look up words in the dictionary. Looking up words in the dictionary was hard. Miss Pepper's dictionary was fat, and it was on a special dictionary stand in the corner. It was hard to make it stay open to the page you wanted. There was so much little print on each page, and it was easy to lose your place while you were looking back at the special place on the blackboard to see the word. If you lost your place, the pages flopped over, and you had to start all over again.

"Today's word is a really difficult one," said Miss Pepper. "Three syllables!"

Miss Pepper went to the blackboard and picked up a piece of chalk. Under the place where it said "Word of the Day," she wrote *palindrome*.

"Who would like to look up this word in the dictionary?" asked Miss Pepper.

She looked around the room and said, "I'll give you a hint." She looked at Hannah.

On the blackboard Miss Pepper wrote, "Hannah is a palindrome."

Hannah was very surprised. She had never seen herself in a sentence before.

"What's a palindrome?" she wondered.

Miss Pepper raised her chalk to write again.

Just then the buzzer rang. That meant Miss Pepper had to go to the principal's office.

"Who would like to be the monitor while I am gone?" she asked.

All the children raised their hands.

Hannah waved her hand round and round in the air. She wiggled a lot in her seat even though "Don't wiggle" was one of Miss Pepper's *Rules of Good Behavior*. But she wanted to be monitor so much. She also wanted to win a cherry or a licorice fruit drop, even though she couldn't decide which.

"Hannah," said Miss Pepper, "you have always been a conscientious student who follows the rules, except for sometimes when you get the giggles. Being monitor is serious business. It means being the teacher when the teacher is away. If you're sure you wouldn't get the giggles, there is no reason why you shouldn't get a chance to be monitor." She looked at Hannah's note and added, "Also, it would be good practice for you."

Hannah almost flew into Miss Pepper's big chair in front of Miss Pepper's big desk.

"Now I know you will all be quiet and do your word work till I get back," said Miss Pepper. "But if anyone breaks a rule of good behavior, Hannah, just write that person's name on the blackboard."

Then Miss Pepper left the room.

As soon as the door closed, Otto made a loud noise. Otto always made noises when Miss Pepper left the room.

"Stop that, Otto," said Hannah. "You know the rules of good behavior in this classroom."

"Hannah is a palindrome!" said Otto.

"Oh, I am not," Hannah wanted to say. But it was written right on the blackboard.

Hannah wondered what a palindrome was. She didn't want Otto to know she didn't know.

"No talking out, Otto!" said Hannah. "That's one of the rules and you know it. Who will look up today's word in the dictionary?"

"Hannah is a palindrome!" said Otto.

"That's enough fooling around now, Otto," said Hannah.

She picked up a piece of chalk and wrote "Otto Zimmer" on the blackboard. She wrote with her best penmanship because "Don't write with poor penmanship" was another one of Miss Pepper's rules. While Hannah was writing, the chalk squeaked.

"Eek!" said Otto, imitating the chalk.

"You want me to write your name down twice?" asked Hannah.

"Hannah is a palindrome!" said Otto.

"Otto! *No talking*!" said Hannah. "That's the most important rule!"

All Miss Pepper's rules were important, like "No getting the giggles, because you could pass it on to your neighbor," and "Never waste paper on a paper airplane and, if you do, don't sail it."But some rules were more important than others. "No talking" was the most important rule of all.

All of a sudden other kids were talking too.

"No talking!" said Hannah to the class. "I *mean* it. Now who is going to look up that word?"

But the kids who were talking kept right on talking.

"I'll give you one more chance," said Hannah.

But they kept right on talking.

"Hannah is a palindrome!" said Willie Hoffman.

Melba Pringle and Tessie Simon said it right after him.

So Hannah wrote, "Willie Hoffman," "Melba Pringle," and "Tessie Simon" right under "Otto Zimmer."

Then Alfred Hennessy made a little paper airplane and sailed it across the room at Becky Jackson.

"No paper airplanes, Alfred," said Hannah. "Now who is going to look up that word?"

Becky Jackson sailed the little paper airplane back at Alfred Hennessy.

"Listen, Alfred and Becky," said Hannah, "I *mean* it. Stop sailing little airplanes."

So they made and sailed medium-sized ones instead.

Hannah added their names to the ones on the blackboard.

Then she turned around and said, "Who is going to look up that word?"

Nobody answered.

They all started to talk, giggle, and sail airplanes.

Hannah clapped her hands together loudly, as Miss Pepper did when the room got too noisy. She even said, "This is disgraceful behavior!" the way Miss Pepper did, but no one heard her. They were too busy talking, giggling, and making and sailing paper airplanes. Hannah didn't feel one bit like giggling. She felt like putting on her coat, walking

out of the room, and going home. But there was another rule, "Don't give up the ship." It means "Keep trying."

So Hannah didn't give up the ship. She wanted Miss Pepper to say, "Well done," when she came back into the room, as she did to the other good monitors.

"Hannah is a palindrome!" yelled Otto.

Then everybody in the room said it with him.

Hannah wrote more names on the blackboard. Her right arm was getting tired. Her penmanship was getting harder to read.

"I don't like being monitor so much," she thought. She wished Miss Pepper would hurry up and come back and say, "This is disgraceful behavior!" to the rest of the class and "Well done, Hannah." Besides, there wasn't any more room on the blackboard to write more names. Also, there weren't any names left to write. Hannah had written the name of every kid in the class.

"Miss Pepper will disapprove of their behavior," she thought. "They'll really get it when she comes back. Wait — maybe *I'll* get it. Maybe Miss Pepper will say, 'Why didn't you keep them quiet?' Maybe I won't get a cherry *or* a licorice fruit drop."

"Who is going to look up that word?" said Hannah one more time. But she knew no one would answer.

"This is terrible," she said to herself. "How will I ever be a teacher? No one is even listening to me. I can't decide what to do."

Hannah walked over to the dictionary. No one even noticed her. She looked up *palindrome*. She read for a long time.

After she had finished looking in the dictionary, she looked at Otto. She closed the dictionary and picked it up. It was very heavy.

Hannah carried it to Miss Pepper's desk.

"*Quiet!*" she said. "I looked up the word myself. I'm *telling* you something!"

Hannah slammed the big heavy dictionary down on Miss Pepper's desk. It made such a loud bang, even Hannah jumped. Otto's lower jaw flopped open.

And the room got quiet. The airplanes stopped. The kids sat down and stared at Hannah.

She picked up all the airplanes. She erased all the names so she would have room to write.

She picked up a new piece of chalk. Underneath where Miss Pepper had written the new word, Hannah wrote, "Otto is a palindrome."

She wrote slowly and carefully. The chalk didn't squeak.

Otto's mouth fell open even wider.

Hannah turned around and faced the class.

"A palindrome," she said, "is a word that is spelled the same backward as forward. Now write *palindrome* five times, and for homework use it in a sentence."

The room was very quiet.

The door opened and Miss Pepper walked in. She looked all around.

"Why, what a lovely class," she said. "How nice it makes me feel to think you were so well behaved and quiet while I was gone. Not one name on the blackboard. And 'Otto is a palindrome'! Why, I was just about to write that on the blackboard myself when the buzzer rang. How clever of you to figure that out by yourself, Hannah. What a good teacher you are. Well done, Hannah. Would you like a licorice or a cherry fruit drop?"

Hannah couldn't answer. All of a sudden she felt very tired. She went back to her seat and sat down. She put her head down on top of her desk. Inside the circle of her arms, she did some thinking. "What should I tell her?" she wondered. "I can't be dishonest." She was ashamed to accept a fruit drop. Also, she still hadn't decided which flavor.

So she took out a piece of paper and wrote Miss Pepper another note.

She wrote:

Dear Miss Pepper,

It wasn't really quiet while you were gone. People talked and yelled and sailed airplanes.

I clapped my hands and stamped my feet and wrote all the names on the blackboard. There wasn't any more room to write so I had to erase.

Nobody would look up <u>palindrome</u> in the dictionary. So I looked it up. That's how I figured out about Otto.

I didn't giggle, but I slammed the dictionary down on your desk. It made a big bang. Everybody jumped. I jumped too. And that's how it finally got quiet, just before you came in the door.

I was a terrible monitor. I'll never be able to be a teacher.

Love,
Hannah

P.S. Do I still get the fruit drop?

Hannah went up to the pencil sharpener again and sharpened her pencil till there was almost nothing left. She dropped the note on Miss Pepper's desk on her way back to her seat.

Miss Pepper read the note.

When she finished, she said, "Well, of all things! Hannah, this sounds just like a description of what happened to me on the very first day of the very first year I was a teacher! I know exactly how that feels. I slammed a book down like that myself! That's when I started to make Miss Pepper's *Rules of Good Behavior.* Now if there's one thing I really like it's an honest person!

"You used your ingenuity — and that will be the new word for tomorrow. Would you like to clap the erasers together now, Hannah? And would you like a cherry or a licorice fruit drop?"

Hannah stared at Miss Pepper. She had never heard her teacher say things like that before. She couldn't believe it!

After a while, Hannah got up. She took the erasers over to the window. She opened the window and clapped erasers together two at a time. She looked up and watched the chalk clouds float up toward the real clouds. The sky was bright, blue, and beautiful.

When all the chalk dust was gone, Hannah closed the window. She put the erasers back and went over to Miss Pepper's desk.

She looked at the little box that said "Licorice," then at the little box that said "Cherry."

"I've made a decision," said Hannah. "I'll have one of each, please."

Author

Mindy Warshaw Skolsky began writing stories for her students when she was a teacher. She has continued to write them for her own children. Mrs. Skolsky sees writing as a lovely opportunity to tell stories to children. There are several books about Hannah and her adventures.

Comprehension Questions

1. Do you think Hannah was a good class monitor?
2. What problem did Hannah have that she didn't expect a monitor to have?
3. How did Hannah get the students to be quiet?
4. What did Hannah find out about the word *palindrome*? Why did she say that Otto is a palindrome?

Vocabulary

The words below name some of the things you might find in a classroom. Can you name some other important things in *your* classroom?

desks	**pencils**	**chalkboard**	**chalk**
erasers	**chairs**	**dictionary**	**windows**

Use the words above and other appropriate words to describe your classroom.

Writing a Paragraph

Miss Pepper's "new word for tomorrow" was *ingenuity*. Look up *ingenuity* in the Glossary. Then write a paragraph telling how Hannah used her ingenuity to quiet the class.

Palindromes

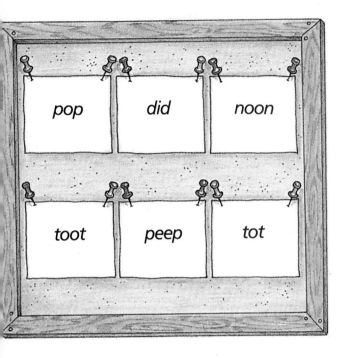

Read the words on the signs above. Now read the words backwards. These words say the same thing whether you read them forwards or backwards. They are **palindromes**.

Think of a palindrome to finish each sentence at the top of the next column. One letter is missing from each palindrome. On a separate paper, write the palindromes.

Nose is not a palindrome, but e___e is.

Napkin is not a palindrome, but baby's b___b is.

Kitten is not a palindrome, but p___p is.

Sometimes words together can be a palindrome. Read these words: *wet stew.* Now read them backwards. Pause at the line: *wet s/tew.* Can you find the palindromes in the list below? On a separate paper, write the palindromes.

evil olive   fast pack
put up   gold log

Even sentences can be palindromes. Can you tell which of the sentences below is a palindrome?

Who ate the beef stew?
Which blue hat is yours?
Was it a cat I saw?

181

Ramón and the Pirate Gull

by Robert Barry

One day at the beach, Ramón finds a very unusual bird. He thinks it may be a pirate gull. Find out who else is interested in this strange bird and why.

182

Ramón's kite rose higher and higher in the morning sky. He let the string slip slowly through his fingers, as he stood on the beach in the soft, drowsy warmth of the morning sun. He closed his eyes.

Even without looking, he could tell by the string's pull on his hand when the kite was tossing to the left or to the right, and when it was about to swoop and slice a big circle in the bright Caribbean sky.

Suddenly, a strange, laughing sound pierced the air. *Haah, haah, haah* . . . Ramón opened his eyes. He blinked them at a bright flash of red. High overhead, a bird posed briefly, then dove straight down at a pelican that was fishing lazily in the waters of the bay.

The bird landed lightly on the pelican's head. Ramón gasped. It was a bright red gull! When the pelican opened its huge beak, the gull darted in with its head and speared a fish out of the pelican's pouch. Then it sailed away into the sky.

Ramón held his breath with amazement as the red gull came back again and again to perch on the pelican's head and snatch more fish. Ramón counted two, four, five, six fish! At last there was only one fish left in the pelican's pouch. Gull and pelican fought a brief tug-of-war. The gull won. Swiftly it flew away

with its prize, disappearing over the palm trees that lined the edge of the beach.

Ramón shook his head and hauled in his kite as quickly as he could. He ran along the path to the clearing where his house stood.

"A sea gull . . . a sea gull as red as a ruby. I saw it at the beach," he cried.

"What are you shouting about, Ramón?" his mother asked, coming out onto the porch. "You know that sea gulls aren't red. Maybe you saw a crane. I have seen pictures of pink cranes with long legs."

"Yes, it's true," Ramón insisted and tried to catch his breath. "I saw a red sea gull stealing fish from a pelican . . . just like a pirate."

"Ramón, come in now," his mother said. "Have your breakfast and tell me more about this bird."

But Ramón could not eat. He was too excited to sit still. He raced off into town and went straight to the plaza. Near the fountain, he saw his friend Flora, who sold fruit. Ramón tried to tell her about the red gull, but Flora said, "Ramón, I've seen red fish, but there's no such thing as a red gull."

Ramón met another friend, Miguel, who sold newspapers.

"The gull was red as fire and could do as many tricks as my kite," he told him.

Miguel laughed and said, "Ramón, if there were a red gull here in Ponce, Puerto Rico, its picture would be in color on the front page of the newspaper."

Ramón walked to the other side of the plaza, where the island taxis were parked. There Carlos was painting some words on a window of his taxi, which he drove daily from Ponce to San Juan. "It will say 'Wheels of Fire,'" he told Ramón, as he stepped back to admire his work.

"Carlos, what would you say if I told you that I saw a sea gull this morning . . . a gull as red as the engine in the firehouse?"

"I would say that it was something that you saw in a dream," Carlos answered.

Ramón persisted. "It was laughing and stealing fish from a pelican."

Carlos put his brush down. "Ramón, if you go on with that story, you'll make me spill this paint. My hand is shaking enough already."

Ramón sighed. How could he prove that he'd seen a red gull?

He stopped to look at the waves as he walked back home. The pelican was gone, and the beach was deserted. Then Ramón heard the sound again. . . . *Haah . . . haah. . . .*

It came from the other side of some rocks that stood out in the water. Ramón scrambled over the slippery boulders. The gull was there, bright and red, fluttering among the rocks. It had a ruffled place on one of its wings and couldn't fly. "That pelican must have hurt you," Ramón said. He reached down and carefully picked up the gull. "I'll take you home, little pirate, and see if I can patch you up."

"That bird looks like a birthday package," Ramón's mother said, looking down into the box that Ramón was making into a comfortable nest. "It's a gull, but I've never seen a red gull before."

The bird stretched and combed its feathers. "If I let you go before you can fly, a big cat will get you," Ramón told it. "I will keep you until you are strong again. Then I will let you go."

Just then, he heard Flora calling, "Ramón, Ramón!" She was running toward the house, and Miguel and Carlos were following her. "Ramón, THE BIRD IS WANTED! There's a picture of it at the post office. If you have seen a red sea gull, you must report it to The Marine Research Station in San Juan!"

"It must be wanted for stealing fish," said Miguel.

"No," denied Carlos. "It could be a rare bird that is wanted for the zoo."

Ramón's mother looked concerned. "You must take the gull to The Marine Research Station in San Juan, Ramón. It is injured, and they'll know what to do with it there."

"I will take you in my taxi," Carlos volunteered. "We can leave whenever you are ready."

Ramón's mother said, "I'll come with you. It's about time I visited my cousin Carmen in San Juan, anyhow."

A crowd gathered in the plaza to see Ramón leave with his mother and Carlos. There were police officers, taxi drivers, shoppers, and storekeepers . . . even the Mayor had heard about the strange bird that was found in Ponce. They all cheered as Carlos drove off with a roar. Ramón and his mother waved from the taxi, and the red gull flapped its wings.

Carlos drove east along the coast to Salinas. The taxi passed coconut groves and fields of waving sugar cane as Carlos turned north. Then they started to drive up the mountain.

After a long and bumpy ride, they arrived in San Juan. Carlos steered the taxi through the narrow streets of the city and parked at The Marine Research Station. There, Ramón lifted the sea gull out of the box and carried it into the building. His mother and Carlos followed him.

"You must want to see Señora Santiago," the lady at the desk said when she saw the red bird in Ramón's arms. She led them to an office at the end of a hallway. "Señora Santiago," she said to a woman seated at a desk. "Here is one of the gulls you are looking for."

"I found it on the beach in Ponce," Ramón reported. "It has injured its wing."

"Well, that looks like one of our gulls, but we did not expect to have it delivered . . . like this," Señora Santiago said, smiling.

"It is one of several gulls that were marked with a red dye to help us trace their winter migration routes," she continued. "This one has traveled all the way from Woods Hole in Massachusetts" — she pointed to a big map on the wall — "to here." Her finger stopped at Puerto Rico. "It has come very far. Why don't you put this red pin into the map next to the town of Ponce," she said, giving a pin to Ramón.

"You mean," Carlos inquired, "that this gull is not a thief who is wanted for stealing fish from pelicans?"

"Of course not," Señora Santiago replied. "This is a *laughing gull*. Taking fish from pelicans is just one of its habits. *Laughing gulls* are clever enough to let

other birds fish for them. If you leave the gull with us, we'll see that it is cared for. As for the red dye, it will disappear when the gull sheds its old feathers and grows new ones."

"So the gull is part of an experiment," said Ramón's mother, nodding her head. "It is not a thief, after all."

"The red dye will be gone in a few months," said Carlos.

"That gull will be flying again soon . . . and stealing fish too," added Ramón.

"We must be going now," Carlos said. "We have a long trip back to Ponce."

They all said good-by, and Ramón shook hands with Señora Santiago.

It had been a long exciting day for Ramón. As the taxi started to climb the mountain road, he curled up in the back seat and fell asleep. He did not even remember arriving back at his house near the beach.

Author

A native of Rhode Island, Robert Barry spent ten years living in San Juan, Puerto Rico, where he was part owner of an art business. He knows firsthand the background of Ramón's story. Among other books by Mr. Barry is *Mr. Willowby's Christmas Tree*, a funny story about a wealthy man and the animals who borrowed his tree.

The Red Gull's Journey

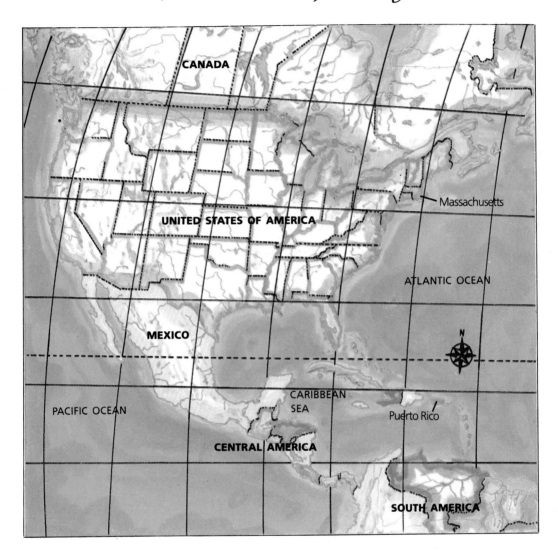

Using a Compass Rose

In which direction did the red gull travel to get to Ponce, Puerto Rico? Use the compass rose to answer this question.

Comprehension Questions

1. Who else was interested in the sea gull that Ramón found? Why?
2. Why did Ramón call the gull a pirate?
3. Do you think Ramón will tell his friends if he sees other birds with unusual colors? Why or why not?

Vocabulary

The words below were used to describe how the gull took fish from the pelican. Use one word in place of the blank in each sentence. Then complete the sentence.

sailed   **dove**   **speared**   **snatch**

1. The gull _____ down at a pelican that was . . .
2. The gull _____ a fish out of . . .
3. The gull _____ away into the sky after . . .
4. The gull returned to _____ more fish. It took . . .

Writing a Report

Pretend that you were at The Marine Research Station when Ramón returned the gull. Write a report telling how the sea gull was found and returned.

Sea Shopping

by Bette Killion

Low tide
   and the beach becomes
The sea's department store
   of treasures:
Conch shells, cat's eyes,
   olives, and sundials,
Sea stars, sand dollars,
   and a host of
White-to-brown little ones —
All crowding the bargain counters.

What do we pay
   for these treasures?
That's the lovely part!
Just a smile and a wave
   to the swooping gulls,
A race on the sands
   with a sandpiper,
A shriek of joy when the tide
   catches us unaware —
The shells are free to enjoy.

Making Inferences

Every day people give you information that you need to think about. Or someone asks you for information about something and you have to think of an answer. Have you ever thought about how you think?

When you think, sometimes you put two or more facts together from what you read or hear. At other times you put together information that you read or hear with knowledge that you already have. When you do this, you are making an inference.
Read this:

> Tony said, "Ed, come to my house for breakfast at 9 o'clock. After we have breakfast, we can go outside to play and then Mother will drive us to the library."

Think about the answers to the questions at the top of the next page and about how you knew the answers.

1. Will Ed go to Tony's house in the morning, afternoon, or evening?
2. What kinds of things might Tony and Ed have to eat when Ed comes to Tony's house?
3. Are Tony and Ed children or adults?
4. What might Tony and Ed bring back from the place to which Tony's mother is driving them?
5. What do you think Tony and Ed might do after they come from the library?

You can't be *sure* about the answers to all five of the questions. If you were thinking, you probably had pretty good ideas for most of the answers. None of the answers can be found in the words you've read. Here are some answers you may have thought about for two of the questions.

1. It will be morning when Ed goes to Tony's home. The story didn't say it was morning, but the story did say that it would be 9 o'clock and that they would have breakfast. You can put together two facts from the story because you know that breakfast is a morning meal.
2. Tony and Ed might eat eggs or bacon or toast. The boys will be eating breakfast, and you can think about the kinds of things you know that people usually eat for breakfast.

Now that you've read about how you make inferences, be ready to tell how you thought about the answers to questions 3, 4, and 5.

Now read below, one sentence at a time. Try to guess what the person is thinking about.

It's a letter of the alphabet.
The letter is in the first half of the alphabet.
The letter is after the letter *i*.
The letter is before the letter *k*.

After the first clue you did not know just which letter the person was thinking of, but you could have made a guess.

The second clue got you closer to the answer. You know about alphabetical order. You know that a letter in the first half of the alphabet could be any letter from *a* through *m*. You now also know that any letter in the last half of the alphabet is no longer a possible answer.

The third clue got you even closer. You needed to put together the fact that it is a letter, the fact that it is a letter in the first half of the alphabet, but also a letter after *i*. Now the only possible answers are *j*, *k*, *l*, and *m*.

The last clue helped you think of the exact answer. There are lots of letters before the letter *k*, but if you put together the fact that the letter comes after *i* and the fact that it comes before *k*, you know that the letter is *j*. *J* is the only letter between *i* and *k*.

Making Inferences

Now read below, one sentence at a time. Be ready to tell how you knew the answer.

> I am thinking of a number.
> The number is less than 50.
> The number is more than 40.
> The number is less than 42.

Skill Summary

When you make an inference:

- Sometimes you need to put together two or more facts to figure out something.
- Sometimes you need to put together facts you read or hear with knowledge you already have.

What Makes a Bird a Bird?

by May Garelick

There's something special about birds that makes
them different from any other kind of animal.
What is that something special?

200

In trees and in bushes, on the ground, and in the air, birds are flying, singing, calling, and nesting.

How do we know that a bird is a bird? What makes it different from any other type of animal? What makes a bird unique?

Is a bird unique because it flies? A fly flies, and so do butterflies, ladybugs, dragonflies, and bees. But these animals are not birds. They are insects.

Many insects fly. They do not fly as fast as birds, but many insects do fly.

And what is this furry-looking creature, flying around in the middle of the night? It's not an insect, and it's not a bird. It's a bat.

Bats sleep during the day, hanging upside-down in hollow trees or in caves. At night they fly around, trying to catch insects for food.

Bats, insects, and birds are not the only animals that fly.

What do you think this creature is, flying above the water? Is it a bat? An insect? A bird? No, it's a flying fish that has been frightened by an enemy under water. Like all fish, flying fish live most of the time in water. If an enemy comes

Bat in flight

Four-winged flying fish

Domestic rooster

Penguin with outstretched wings

near, however, a flying fish can jump up out of the water, glide through the air, and escape.

If there are flying insects, flying bats, and even flying fish, then it is not flying that makes a bird unique. As a matter of fact, you know a bird that doesn't really fly.

Have you ever seen a chicken fly? Sometimes a chicken attempts to fly, but it doesn't get far. To get anywhere, a chicken walks. Is a chicken a bird? Yes.

Can you think of another bird that can't fly? Penguins cannot fly; they walk. Down to the water they waddle and into the sea for a swim. Penguins are excellent swimmers. They use their flipper-like wings to paddle through the water.

Another bird that cannot fly is the ostrich, the biggest bird in the world. Although it can't fly, the ostrich's long legs make it a very swift runner. An ostrich can run as fast as forty miles an hour.

If ostriches, penguins, and chickens cannot fly, what makes them birds? Are they birds because they have wings?

Birds definitely have wings, but look at a fly flying around. You can see its wings. Dragonflies, butterflies, and bees have wings too. If some insects have wings, then it is not wings that make a bird unique.

Is a bird a bird because it sings? Birds sing and call messages to each other, especially in the spring. That's how birds communicate with one another.

One bird's song may be a warning to other birds to keep away. Usually the other birds will keep away. If they don't, there may be a fight.

Butterfly resting on flowers

A mother hen clucks to her chicks to tell them that there is food. The chicks recognize her call and come running for the food.

A duck quacks to signal her ducklings to follow her. Baby robins make peeping sounds to let their parents know they are hungry.

Birds sing and call messages to each other, but many insects communicate by singing and calling. Crickets chirp, and grasshoppers hum. Katydids repeat their rhythmic song all night long.

If there are insects that can sing and call, then it is not singing and calling that make a bird unique. What *is* the special thing that makes a bird a bird?

Drone fly on flower

Whippoorwill with eggs on leaves

Is a bird unique because it builds a nest? Birds build nests in trees, in bushes, under eaves, and in barns. They build nests wherever their eggs and their babies will be safe.

Some birds, however, build no nests at all. A whippoorwill lays her eggs among the leaves on the ground.

Birds are not the only animals that build nests. Ants, bees, snakes, fish, rabbits, mice, and other animals make nests too.

Red-winged blackbird's eggs and nest

If other animals build nests, then it is not nest building that makes a bird a bird.

Egg laying is not what makes a bird unique, either. It's true that all birds lay eggs, but so do frogs, snakes, fish, bees, mosquitoes, and many other animals.

So — it isn't flying that makes a bird different from anything else alive.

And it's not having wings.

And it's not singing or calling.

And it's not building nests or laying eggs.

What is it, then, that makes a bird a bird?

Birds have something that no other living thing has. What is it?

A large group of lorikeets decorates tree branches with brilliant colors.

Feather of red-tailed hawk

Peacock with outstretched wings

FEATHERS! Only birds have feathers. That's the special thing that makes a bird unique. A bird has to have feathers to be a bird. Whether it flies or not, any animal with feathers is a bird.

Feathers are strong. Try to break or tear one, and you'll see how strong a feather is. Bend a feather so the tip touches the bottom. Watch it spring back. It won't break.

Feathers are light. Hold a feather, and you'll see how light it is. You've probably heard people say that something is "light as a feather."

Feathers are beautiful, and they come in many colors. There are feathers from red cardinals, blue jays, blackbirds, white doves, green parrots, brown sparrows, and many other colored birds.

Feathers are useful too. They do many things for birds. Feathers make birds the best flyers. Even though some other animals fly, no living creature can fly as long or as far as a bird.

Feathers also help keep birds warm in winter. Watch a bird on a cold day. It looks like a fat puffball because it has fluffed out all its feathers to keep out the cold.

Feathers help keep birds dry in the rain. Put a drop of water on a feather, and watch the water slide off.

Birds take good care of their feathers by cleaning and smoothing them with their beaks. This is called *preening*. Most birds also oil their feathers while they preen. They get the oil from their tails. When they apply it to their feathers, it waterproofs and softens the feathers.

Small green heron preening itself

Most birds also bathe to keep their feathers clean. Some birds bathe in water, and others bathe in fine dust. However, no matter how well birds clean their feathers, they get brittle and wear out. At least once a year, birds *molt* — their worn-out feathers fall out. Birds don't shed all their feathers at once, just one or two at a time. As the old feathers fall out, new ones grow in.

You may find some of these old feathers on the ground. Pick them up and look at them.

Feathers are the special things that make a bird a bird.

Bald eagle in flight

Author

Russian-born May Garelick has worked in many different publishing jobs. She has written a number of children's books. Most are about nature or science, and several are about birds. Ms. Garelick says, "I like to ask a question in each of my books to encourage readers to make their own discoveries in nature and in the world around them."

Thinking It Over

Comprehension Questions

1. What is special about birds that makes them different from other animals?
2. What does *unique* mean?
3. What are some ways in which birds are *like* other animals?
4. Why do you think an ostrich cannot fly?
5. Name three animals besides birds that build nests and lay eggs.

Vocabulary

The article you have just read talked about many animals. Use the words in the box in sentences that tell about some of the animals. Look again at the article if you need help.

hollow	**waddle**	**swift**	**rhythmic**
glide	**paddle**	**clucks**	**chirp**

Making a Chart

You read about many animals other than birds in this article. Make a chart to show how the animals are like birds. Use the following headings: *flying, wings, singing and calling, building nests, laying eggs*. List under each heading the animals that have or do those things.

Flying	Wings	Singing and Calling	Building Nests	Laying Eggs

Science Words

There are many words we can use to describe animals. Here are some of them:

den   Home of a wild animal.

feathers   Light special parts that grow out of a bird's skin.

fur   Thick, soft hair that covers some animals.

groom   To make neat.

molt   To lose the outer covering.

nest   A home made by birds to hold their eggs.

preen   To smooth or clean feathers with a beak.

shed   To lose an outer covering in a natural way.

Read the paragraph below.

You probably think that birds and lions are as different as can be. But a lion **grooms** its **fur** just as a bird **preens** its **feathers**. Lions **shed** their fur, and birds lose their feathers when they **molt**. A mother lion does not build a **nest**. But she does make a cozy **den** that is safe and warm for her cubs.

Which four words in the paragraph tell about birds? Which four words tell about lions?

Now use the words from the paragraph to finish the rhyme on page 211. Look back at the glossary on this page if you need help with their meanings. On a separate paper, copy the rhyme using the words you have chosen.

I _____ my feathers so I'm neat as a pin.

As my old feathers _____, new _____ grow in.

I build my _____ out of twigs and string.

Worms for breakfast really make me sing.

I _____ my fur so I'm clean and neat.

I _____ some _____ in the summertime heat.

I live in a _____ where I sleep all day.

I roar when I'm happy and growl when I play.

Something Extra

Groups of animals have special names. A group of birds is a *flock of birds*. A group of lions is a *pride of lions*.

Young animals have special names too. A baby bird is a *chick*. A baby lion is a *cub*.

Read about some other animals. Then make a poster for a favorite animal. Draw the animal's picture at the top and write its name. Then list the kind of outer covering it has, where it lives, what it is called as a group, and what it is called as a baby.

LION

Covering: fur
Home: den

Group: pride
Baby: cub

Miss Rumphius

by Barbara Cooney

When Miss Rumphius was a little girl, there were three special things she wanted to do when she grew up. What were the three special things? Did she do them?

The Lupine Lady lives in a small house overlooking the sea. In between the rocks around her house grow blue and purple and rose-colored flowers. The Lupine Lady is very old. But she has not always been that way. I know. She is my great-aunt, and she told me so.

Once upon a time she was a little girl named Alice who lived in a city by the sea. From the front stoop she could see the wharves and the masts of tall ships.

Many years earlier, Alice's grandfather had come to America on a large sailing ship. Now he worked in the shop at the bottom of his house and made figureheads for the prows of ships. For Alice's grandfather was an artist. He painted pictures, too, of sailing ships and places across the sea. When he was very busy, Alice helped him put in the skies.

In the evening, Alice sat on her grandfather's knee and listened to his stories of faraway places. When he had finished, Alice would say, "When I grow up, I too will go to faraway places, and when I grow old, I too will live beside the sea."

"That is all very well, little Alice," said her grandfather, "but there is a third thing you must do."

"What is that?" asked Alice.

"You must do something to make the world more beautiful," said her grandfather.

"All right," said Alice, but she did not know what that could be.

In the meantime, Alice got up and washed her face and ate porridge for breakfast. She went to school and came home and did her homework.

And pretty soon she was grown up.

Then my great-aunt Alice set out to do the three things she had told her grandfather she was going to do. She left home and went to live in another city far from the sea and the salt air. There she worked in a library, helping people find the books they wanted. Some of the books told her about faraway places.

People called her Miss Rumphius now.

Sometimes she went to the conservatory in the middle of the park. When she stepped inside on a wintry day, the warm, moist air wrapped itself around her, and the sweet smell of jasmine filled her nose.

"This is almost like a tropical isle," said Miss Rumphius, "but not quite."

So Miss Rumphius went to a real tropical island. She walked on long beaches, picking up beautiful shells.

In one fishing village she was given a beautiful shell on which was painted a golden bird and the words, "You will always remain in our hearts."

"You will always remain in mine too," said Miss Rumphius.

My great-aunt Miss Alice Rumphius climbed tall mountains where the snow never melted. She went through jungles and across deserts. She saw lions playing and kangaroos jumping. And everywhere she made friends she would never forget. Finally she went to Africa. There, getting down off a camel, she hurt her back.

"What a foolish thing to do," said Miss Rumphius. "Well, I have certainly seen faraway places. Maybe it is time to find my place by the sea."

And it was, and she did.

From the porch of her new house, Miss Rumphius watched the sun come up; she watched it cross the sky and sparkle on the water; and she saw it set in glory in the evening. She started a little garden

among the rocks that surrounded her house, and she planted a few flower seeds in the stony ground. Miss Rumphius was *almost* perfectly happy.

"But there is still one more thing I have to do," she said. "I have to do something to make the world more beautiful."

But what? "The world already is pretty nice," she thought, looking out over the ocean.

The next spring Miss Rumphius was not very well. Her back was bothering her again, and she had to stay in bed most of the time.

The flowers she had planted the summer before had come up and bloomed in spite of the stony ground. She could see them from her bedroom window — blue and purple and rose-colored.

"Lupines," said Miss Rumphius with satisfaction. "I have always loved lupines the best. I wish I could plant more seeds this summer so that I could have still more flowers next year."

But she was not able to.

After a hard winter, spring came. Miss Rumphius was feeling much better. Now she could take walks again. One afternoon, she started to go up and over the hill, where she had not been in a long time.

"I don't believe my eyes!" she cried when she got to the top. For there on the other side of the hill was a large patch of blue and purple and rose-colored lupines!

"It was the wind," she said as she knelt in delight. "It was the wind that brought the seeds from my garden here! And the birds must have helped!"

Then Miss Rumphius had a wonderful idea!

She hurried home and got out her seed catalogs. She sent off to the very best seed house for five bushels of lupine seeds.

All that summer Miss Rumphius, her pockets full of seeds, wandered over fields and headlands, sowing lupines. She scattered the seeds along the highways and down the country lanes. She flung handfuls of them around the schoolhouse. She tossed them into hollows and along stone walls.

Her back didn't hurt her any more at all.

The next spring there were lupines everywhere. Fields and hillsides were covered with blue and purple and rose-colored flowers. They bloomed along the highways and down the lanes. Bright patches of lupines lay around the schoolhouse. Down in the hollows and along the stone walls grew the beautiful flowers.

Miss Rumphius had done the third, the most difficult thing of all!

My great-aunt Alice, Miss Rumphius, is very old
now. Her hair is very white. Every year there are
more and more lupines. Now people call her the
Lupine Lady. Sometimes my friends stand with me
outside her gate, curious to see the old, old lady who
planted the fields of lupines. When she invites us in,
they come slowly. They think she is the oldest woman
in the world. Often she tells us stories of faraway
places.

"When I grow up," I tell her, "I too will go to faraway places and come home to live by the sea."

"That is all very well, little Alice," says my great-aunt, "but there is a third thing you must do."

"What is that?" I ask.

"You must do something to make the world more beautiful."

"All right," I say. But I do not know yet what that can be.

Author

Barbara Cooney is famous as an author and an illustrator. Her books for children have won many awards and honors. *Chanticleer and the Fox* won the Caldecott Medal. *Miss Rumphius*, which you have just read, was the co-winner of the 1983 American Book Award for picture books and was named a Notable Children's Trade Book in Social Studies.

Thinking It Over

Comprehension Questions

1. What were the three special things Miss Rumphius did when she grew up?
2. Where did Miss Rumphius work after she grew up and left home?
3. What caused Miss Rumphius to stop traveling?
4. How did the lupine seeds get to the other side of the hill?
5. Why did the person telling the story say making the world more beautiful was the most difficult thing Miss Rumphius had to do?

Vocabulary

Make up clues about the words in the box. Check the Glossary if you are unsure of the meaning of a word. Ask a friend to guess which word you are thinking of. Then have your friend give some clues and you guess.

figurehead	**stoop**	**isle**
prow	**conservatory**	**catalog**

Writing a Letter

Miss Rumphius sent off to the very best seed house for more lupine seeds. Give the seed house a name and write the letter Miss Rumphius might have written.

THE LIBRARY

by Barbara A. Huff

It looks like any building
When you pass it on the street,
Made of stone and glass and marble,
Made of iron and concrete.

But once inside you can ride
A camel or a train,
Visit Rome, Siam, or Nome,
Feel a hurricane,
Meet a king, learn to sing,
How to bake a pie,
Go to sea, plant a tree,
Find how airplanes fly,
Train a horse, and of course
Have all the dogs you'd like,
See the moon, a sandy dune,
Or catch a whopping pike.
Everything that books can bring
You'll find inside those walls.
A world is there for you to share
When adventure calls.

You cannot tell its magic
By the way the building looks,
But there's wonderment within it,
The wonderment of books.

LIBRARY

Taking Tests

For as long as you go to school, you will be tested. There will be many kinds of tests. The various tests will have questions that you will answer in different ways.

True-False   Sometimes you will be asked to tell whether a statement is true or false.

Example:
The largest bodies of water on the earth are the oceans.

(True)   False

Matching   Sometimes you are asked to match the items in one column with those in the other column.

Example:

State	Capital
_b_ Illinois	a. Austin
_a_ Texas	b. Springfield

Completion   At other times, you will be asked to write the missing word in a blank to complete the sentence.

Example:
To find the meanings of the symbols used on a map or globe we use the ___legend___.

226

Though there are still many other kinds of test questions, the kind you may be asked to answer more often than any other is the *multiple-choice.* In multiple-choice tests, you must choose a correct answer from among several different answers.

Before you even look at the first multiple-choice test item, you must read the directions carefully.

Suppose the directions were:

Directions   Underline the one correct answer.

You are told that there is only *one* correct answer and that you are to show your choice by underlining. This means that all the other answer choices are wrong.

Suppose the directions were:

Directions   Write the letter of the one best answer on the blank in front of the numbered question.

Now you are told that more than one answer may be at least partly correct, but you are to choose the *best* one and write its letter on the blank.

What if the directions were:

Directions   Mark *all* of the correct answers for each question by filling in the ovals on your answer sheet.

Now you know that each question may have more than one correct answer. You are to mark the answer sheet to show your answers.

If you don't read the directions carefully, you won't know how to answer the questions and how you are to show your answers. If you do not understand the written directions, ask your teacher.

There are two basic forms of multiple choice items. The first form is an incomplete sentence that leads into the answer choices. Read the incomplete sentence and the answer choices all the way through before choosing an answer. The incomplete sentence together with each answer choice forms a sentence. You must decide which sentence is correct.

Example:

The flowers that Miss Rumphius planted were

a. roses.   c. marigolds.
b. tulips.   d. lupines.

Answer choice *d* is the correct answer.

The second basic form of multiple-choice item is a question followed by multiple, or several, answer choices. Read the question and the answer choices all the way through. Then select the right answer to the question from among the choices.

Example:

Which is another way of writing "four hundred four"?

a. 44   b. 404   c. 4004

Answer choice *b* is the correct answer. How is the first example of multiple-choice item different from the second?

Sometimes you are not to mark your answers on your test. You are to mark them on an answer sheet or card. The test can then be used again by other students, and a computer can be used to score the test.

Below are parts of four answer sheets.

A

	a	b	c	d
1.	::	::	::	::
2.	::	::	::	::
3.	::	::	::	::

B

1. a:: b:: c::
2. a:: b:: c::
3. a:: b:: c::
4. a:: b:: c::

C

1. a:::   2. a:::
   b:::   b:::
   c:::   c:::
   d:::   d:::

D

1. (a) (b) (c)
2. (a) (b) (c)
3. (a) (b) (c)
4. (a) (b) (c)

On A, B, and C, you would show your answer by using your pencil to fill in the space between the lines. On D, you would fill in the oval.

Example:

2. Miss Rumphius hurt her back in

a. South America.   b. Africa.   c. Asia.

If you were to answer the question using answer sheet A, you would first find the space for question *2.* The answer is *b. Africa.* You would blacken the space below the letter *b.*

You may read a multiple-choice item and find that you do not know what the answer really is. You may know what choices could not be correct, but are unsure of the right one. You should not spend too much time on one item. Go through the test and answer the items you are sure of. Then go back and answer the ones you had difficulty with. When you finish the test, check to be sure that you have answered all the items.

Taking a Test

Directions Read the report. Number a paper from 1 to 3. Then beside each number write the letter of your answer choice for that question.

Engine Roundhouses

The engine needs more care than any other part of a train. Years ago, most big railroad yards had round-houses where the engines could be worked on.

The inside of the round-house faced the railroad yard. Between the yard and the roundhouse was a plat-form that was large enough to hold any size engine. The platform was called a turn-table and had on it a single set of tracks.

When the engine was to be taken into the round-

house, it was driven onto the turntable. The turntable was then moved around to meet the tracks that led to an empty stall in the round-house. When both pairs of tracks matched, the engine could be driven into the roundhouse.

Today, an engine that needs repair is separated from the train and driven onto a sidetrack, where the repair work is done. If major repair work is needed, the engine is driven into a workshop.

1. What was kept in the stalls of a roundhouse?

   a. horses
   b. engines
   c. boxcars

2. A roundhouse turntable was

   a. a platform with tracks.
   b. a stall in the round-house.
   c. the inside of the roundhouse.

3. Today an engine is repaired
   a. in a roundhouse.
   b. on a station platform.
   c. on a sidetrack or in a workshop.

Skill Summary

- Before you begin a test, read the directions carefully.
- There are two basic forms of multiple-choice items: (1) an incomplete sentence that leads into answer choices; (2) a question followed by several answer choices.
- You should read all the way through the incomplete sentence or the question and all the answer choices before choosing an answer.
- Sometimes you are to mark your answers on an answer sheet or card instead of on your test paper. Then the test can be used again by other students.

HOW SEEDS TRAVEL

Reading
in
Science:
Textbook

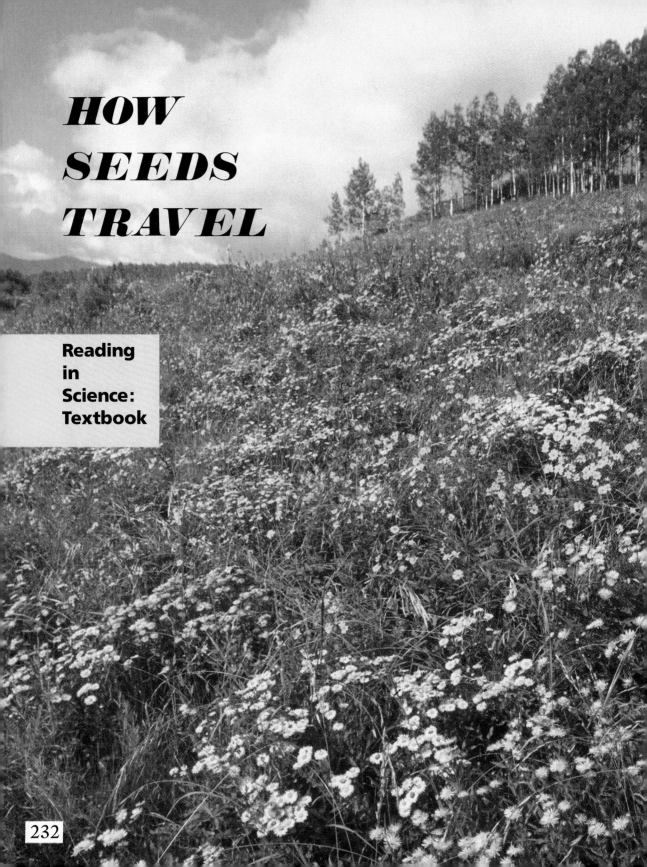

Have you ever tried to grow a plant or a tree? If so, you know that plants need just the right amount of sun and water. They also need good soil and space to grow. Look at the plants on page 232. No one planted them in these places. How did they get there?

These plants all came from seeds that traveled from their parent plants. The parent plant makes seeds inside it. The part of the plant that holds the seeds is called the **fruit**. Some seeds travel inside their fruits. Other seeds travel by themselves. Why do seeds travel?

Seeds travel so that they can live and grow. If all the seeds made by the parent plant fell right under it, they would not have enough room to grow. They would not get enough sun because the parent plant would be blocking the sunlight. How do seeds travel?

Fruits and vegetables with seeds that travel inside fruit — apple, avocado, acorn squash, tomato, grape, peanut, nectarine, green bean

Seeds That Travel by Wind

You know that a very strong wind can pull a tree up by its roots, so you can imagine just how far the wind could carry a tiny seed. Seeds that travel by wind often have special devices that help the wind to carry them. What are some of these special devices?

Some plants, like the columbine, hold their seeds in tubes. When the wind blows, it shakes the seeds out of the tube and carries them away. Other plants, such as the iris, have tiny holes in their fruits. The wind shakes the seeds out of the fruit in much the same way that salt comes out of a salt shaker.

Still other plants have hairs that help the wind carry them. The dandelion is one of these plants. Look at the picture of the ripe dandelion. What looks like a fluffy ball of fur is really hair. The hairs form a kind of parachute at the opposite end of the dandelion fruit. When the air is dry, the hairs of the parachute open and carry the fruit off in the wind. The fruit has tiny **barbs** — points or hooks — all over it. These barbs help the fruit stay on the ground after it lands.

Some plant seeds have wings instead of hairs to

Columbine plants

Ripe dandelion and dandelion flower

234

help them travel by wind. Look at the picture of the maple seeds. Can you see the wings that are attached to each seed? When the wind blows, it pulls the winged seeds off the maple tree. They flutter to the ground. Another wind may carry the seeds some distance away. Then the seeds may ripen and take root.

Elm, ash, and birch trees also have seeds with wings.

Winged maple seeds flutter to the ground when the wind blows.

Seeds That Travel by Water

Have you ever seen water move? Water in lakes, streams, and rivers moves with a current. As the water moves, it may carry seeds with it. How do the seeds get into the water?

Some seeds come from plants that grow near the water. The seeds of these plants fall into the water and are carried to shore where they may take root.

Other seeds may be carried by rainwater or by the wind to a stream or river. Water has been known to carry seeds very great distances.

The coconut is a well-known water traveler. Its fruit is big, but it can stay up in the water because its shell is very light. It is also waterproof.

Seeds That Travel on Animals and People

Have you ever picked a burr off your dog or your clothes? If so, you were helping a plant travel. The fruits of many plants and flowers travel on animals and people.

Look closely at the picture of the **burr** from the great burdock. Can you see all the tiny hooklike parts? These are called **bracts**. They surround the fruit that grows inside. The bracts hook onto people's clothing and onto animals' fur. As the person or animal walks away, the seeds are shaken out of the fruit. They fall to the ground where they may sprout and grow.

Animals help carry fruits and seeds in other ways. Have you ever seen a squirrel gathering acorns? An acorn is actually the fruit of an oak tree. The squirrel may eat part of the nut inside the acorn and let part

Burrs with fruit surrounded by bracts

Squirrel eating acorns

of it fall to the ground. Or, the squirrel may bury the nuts and forget about them. Either way, the seeds of the oak tree are given a chance to sprout and grow.

Birds and other animals often pick fruits, such as berries, and carry them off to be eaten. Often the animals eat only the juicy fruit and let the seeds fall to the ground where they may sprout and grow into new plants.

Display of violets

Seeds That Travel by Scattering Themselves

Not all plants depend on wind, water, people, or animals to carry their seeds. Many plants can scatter their own seeds. How do they do this?

Violets, for example, pop their seeds. Violet seeds grow in three pods that are shaped like canoes. As the seeds grow, the sides of the fruit become dry and squeeze the seeds until they pop. Popped seeds may land several feet away from the parent plant.

Some plants scatter themselves by "walking" away from the parent plant. Of course, plants can't really walk, but they have ways of moving.

The walking fern is one plant that seems to walk away from its parent plant. The leaves of the parent get long and heavy. When they touch the ground, new plants form at the tips of the leaves. These grow into independent plants.

Iowa cornfield with tall corn plants ready to be harvested

Seeds That People Plant

You have seen how many plants travel and grow naturally; however, some plants need people to grow them. Corn is one such plant. It grows only where people plant it. The kernels on an ear of corn are its seeds. The kernels grow tightly together and do not usually fall off where they can sprout. Kernels that do fall to the ground are often eaten by birds and other animals.

Most of the food you eat comes from plants that were grown by people. Every year, farmers plant seeds and care for them until they are fully grown. Then they harvest, or gather, them to be sold for food.

Seeds travel in many different ways. It's a good thing that they do because that makes it possible for plants to grow in many different places.

Questions

Number a paper from 1 to 4. Beside each number write the letter of the correct answer.

1. The part of the plant that holds the seeds is the
   a. root.   c. leaves.
   b. fruit.   d. flower.

2. A seed that travels by wind is the
   a. coconut.   c. corn kernel.
   b. acorn.   d. maple.

3. A plant that has barbs is the
   a. dandelion.
   b. columbine.
   c. violet.
   d. iris.

4. Seeds travel
   a. by wind.
   b. by water.
   c. on people and animals.
   d. by all of the above.

Activity

Not all seeds that fall to the ground take root. Here's how you can find out the number of seeds that may grow from something you plant. Get a large flower box or a cardboard box lined with plastic. Fill the box almost to the top with soft soil. Get a package of seeds, such as cabbage, celery, zinnia, or marigolds. Count the seeds in the package. Then scatter them over the soil. Use a smooth piece of wood to press the seeds into the soil.

Then cover the soil with burlap. Place the box near a sunny window and water the soil every day. After one week, count how many sprouts have come up. Compare this with the number of seeds planted.

The Buried Treasure

**retold by
Djemma Bider**

**illustrated by
Kristina Rodanas**

A man who lives in the mountains has a garden that he loves very much. Caring for the garden takes a great deal of hard work, but the man does not mind working hard.

As the man grows old, he tells his three sons that one day they will inherit the garden. The three brothers are very lazy and do not like hard work. How they come to enjoy working in the garden is a story no one can afford to miss.

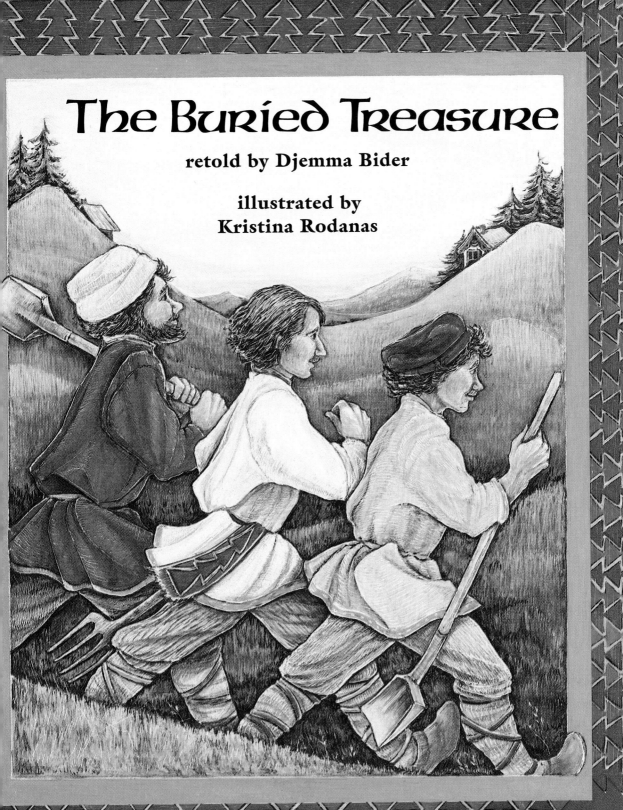

The Buried Treasure

retold by Djemma Bider

illustrated by
Kristina Rodanas

Once upon a time, a man lived in the mountains. He had a garden, and he worked in it all day long. He loved his garden very much.

His three sons loved the garden, too, but they were lazy fellows and did not care for hard work — and hoeing, digging, planting, and carrying water is very hard work.

Still, each of the sons did do something now and then. The oldest son went fishing, the middle

son went hunting, and the youngest son took care of a neighbor's horses. But they did not bring much money home to their families.

The years passed, and one day the father became too old to work. He called his sons to him and said, "Dear children, I will tell you a secret. I happen to know there is a treasure buried in my garden. You will inherit this garden after I die. If you keep digging in the earth, sooner or later you will find the treasure."

Not long after that, the old man died. The sons mourned for their father.

After a while, they gathered their families, relatives, and friends together to discuss what should be done about the treasure in the garden.

"What if we have to dig up the entire garden before we find the treasure?" the oldest son said. "There is no way we can guess where it lies."

"Who knows how deep the treasure is buried? It will be such hard work," said the middle son.

The third son said, "What you say is true, yet how wonderful it would be to find this treasure. We would never have to work again!"

They started to dream aloud . . . .

They would trade some of the gold they found for money and buy wonderful things. When they ran out of money, there would always be enough gold to trade again. All day long they could sit in a café, chatting with friends and drinking tea. What a life it would be!

So they got down to work.

One morning while they were digging, their favorite aunt passed by. "Good day to you, my nephews," she said. "How is it coming along? I wish you good luck."

"It's hard going, dear Aunt," said the oldest son. "We certainly can use your good wishes.

Who knows how long it will take us to find the treasure?"

"Indeed, who knows?" replied the aunt. "But since you are digging in the earth anyway, why don't you plant some seeds? Stop by my house, and I will give you some."

The aunt gave the brothers plenty of seeds: pumpkin and melon seeds, cabbage and carrot seeds, parsley and pea seeds. And she gave them seeds for flowers: marigolds and morning glories, petunias and poppies, sweet williams and snapdragons.

And that was not all. She gave them saplings for apple, plum, apricot, and cherry trees, so that someday they could have an orchard.

The brothers did as their aunt had advised. They planted the seeds as they dug the soil. When they planted the saplings, they made especially deep holes. They watered the soil often.

Day after day, they worked under the hot sun. Their muscles grew stronger, and their skin became so tanned that their teeth and the whites of their eyes sparkled like the snow on the mountaintops. At noontime their children brought

them goat's cheese, flat bread, sour milk, and cakes of rice and honey.

As time passed, the brothers began to love their work. They talked less and less about the treasure; often they forgot the reason they had started digging. The beautiful results of their months of labor began pushing and peeping through the earth.

At summer's end, the brothers had a fine harvest. They brought their vegetables and flowers to the market, and they were the best! Their watermelons were the reddest and ripest. How sweet were their melons — they had a wonderful aroma. And what flowers they sold — people came from faraway mountain villages to buy them.

Year after year, the brothers worked hard in spring and summer, and in autumn they harvested a rich crop. When the villagers celebrated harvest time, the merriest parties were always held at the homes of the three brothers.

And so the three brothers realized how wise their father had been. They understood what their father had meant when he said that sooner or later they would find a treasure in the earth.

Mrs. Morris told the students in her class to form a line. Then she led them to the auditorium. The students were very excited because it was time to try out for parts in the class play. The characters in the play were a young boy, the boy's sister, their parents, friends, neighbors, and a clown. For weeks Jim had practiced for the part he wanted. It was the main part in the play. Now Jim had on a mask that had a red nose and very large red lips. He was quite ready to begin his performance.

1. Jim wanted to be
   a. the young boy.
   b. the clown.
   c. a neighbor.

2. How did you know?
   a. Jim had practiced for weeks.
   b. It was the main part in the play.
   c. Jim had on a mask that had a red nose and large red lips.

Books to Enjoy

A Penguin Year
by Susan Bonner

This award-winning book describes the Adelie penguins of the icy Antarctic.

The Big Balloon Race
by Eleanor Coerr

In an easy-to-read history story, a stowaway girl helps her famous mother win a balloon race.

All the Cats in the World
by Sonia Levitin

The lighthouse keeper makes fun of a woman who feeds homeless cats. Then when the woman is sick, he has a sudden change of heart.

Betsy's Up-and-Down Year
by Anne Pellowski

A Wisconsin girl has both funny and sad adventures in this book about a large farm family.

Journeys
Magazine Three

Contents

Stories

ANNIE AND THE OLD ONE
BY MISKA MILES

Annie, a Navajo girl, lives with her family in the desert. Annie's mother is weaving a rug to sell. Why does Annie decide that her mother must not finish the rug?

Annie's Navajo world was good — a world of rippling sand, of high copper-red bluffs in the distance, of the low mesa near her own snug hogan. The pumpkins were yellow in the cornfield, and the tassels on the corn were turning brown.

Each morning, the gate to the night pen near the hogan was opened wide, and the sheep were herded to pasture on the desert.

Annie helped watch the sheep. She carried pails of water to the cornfield. And every weekday, she walked to the bus stop and waited for the yellow bus that took her to school and brought her home again.

Best of all were the evenings when she sat at her grandmother's feet and listened to stories of times long gone.

Sometimes it seemed to Annie that her grandmother was her age — a girl who had seen no more than nine or ten harvestings.

If a mouse scurried and jerked across the hard dirt floor of their hogan, Annie and her grandmother laughed together. And when they prepared the fried bread for the evening meal, if it burned a bit black at the edges, they laughed and said it was good.

There were other times when her grandmother sat small and still, and Annie knew that she was very old. Then Annie would cover the thin knees of the Old One with a blanket.

It was at such a time that her grandmother said, "It is time you learn to weave, my granddaughter."

Annie touched the web of wrinkles that criss-crossed her grandmother's face and slowly went outside the hogan.

Beside the door, her father sat cross-legged, working with silver and fire, making a handsome, heavy necklace. Annie passed him and went to the big loom where her mother sat weaving.

Annie sat beside the loom watching, while her mother slid the weaving stick in place among the strings of the warp. With red wool, her mother added a row to a slanting arrow of red, bright against the dull background.

Annie's thoughts wandered. She thought about the stories her grandmother had told — stories of hardship when rains flooded the desert — of dry weather when rains did not fall and the pumpkins and corn were dry in the field.

Annie looked out across the sand where the cactus bore its red fruit and thought about the coyote guarding the scattered hogans of the Navajos.

Annie watched while her mother worked. She made herself sit very still.

After a time, her mother looked at her and smiled. "Are you ready to weave now, my daughter?"

Annie shook her head.

She continued to watch while her mother twisted the weaving stick in the warp, making a shed for the strands of gray and red wool.

At last her mother said softly, "You may go," almost as though she knew what Annie wanted.

Annie ran off to find her grandmother, and together they gathered twigs and brush to feed the small fire in the middle of the hogan.

When the evening meal was done, the old grandmother called her family together.

Annie and her mother and father stood quietly, respectfully, waiting for the grandmother to speak.

A coyote called shrilly from the mesa.

There was no sound in the hogan except a small snap of the dying fire.

Then the grandmother spoke softly.

"My children, when the new rug is taken from the loom, I will go to Mother Earth."

Annie shivered and looked at her mother.

Her mother's eyes were shining bright with tears that did not fall, and Annie knew what her grandmother meant. Her heart stood still, and she made no sound.

The Old One spoke again.

"You will each choose the gift that you wish to have."

Annie looked at the hard earth, swept smooth and clean.

"What will you have, my granddaughter?" the grandmother asked.

Annie looked at a weaving stick propped against the wall of the hogan. This was her grandmother's own weaving stick, polished and beautiful with age. Annie looked directly at the stick.

As though Annie had spoken, her grandmother nodded.

"My granddaughter shall have my weaving stick."

On the floor of the hogan lay a rug that the Old One had woven long, long ago. Its colors were soft, and its warp and weft were strong.

Annie's mother chose the rug.

Annie's father chose the silver and turquoise belt that was now loose around the small waist of the Old One.

Annie folded her arms tightly across her stomach and went outside, and her mother followed.

"How can my grandmother know she will go to Mother Earth when the rug is taken from the loom?" Annie asked.

"Many Old Ones know," her mother said.

"How do they know?"

"Your grandmother is one of those who live in harmony with all nature — with earth, coyote, birds in the sky. They know more than many will ever learn. Those Old Ones know." Her mother sighed deeply. "We will speak of other things."

In the days that followed, the grandmother went about her work as she had always done.

She ground corn to make meal for bread.

She gathered dry twigs and brush to make fire.

And when there was no school, she and Annie watched the sheep and listened to the sweet, clear music of the bell on the collar of the lead goat.

The weaving of the rug was high on the loom. It was almost as high as Annie's waist.

"My mother," Annie said, "why do you weave?"

"I weave so we may sell the rug and buy the things we must have from the trading post. Silver for silver-making. Deer hide for boots — "

"But you know what my grandmother said — "

Annie's mother did not speak. She slid her weaving stick through the warp and picked up a strand of rose-red wool.

Annie turned and ran. She ran across the sand and huddled in the shade of the small mesa. Her grand-

mother would go back to the earth when the rug was taken from the loom. The rug must not be finished. Her mother must not weave.

A Part of the Earth

The next morning, where her grandmother went, Annie followed.

When it was time to go to the bus stop to meet the school bus, she dawdled, walking slowly and watching her feet. Perhaps she would miss the bus.

And then quite suddenly she did not want to miss it. She knew what she must do.

She ran hard, as fast as she could — breathing deeply — and the yellow bus was waiting for her at the stop.

She climbed aboard. The bus moved on, stopping now and then at hogans along the way. Annie sat there alone and made her plan.

In school she would be bad, so bad that the teacher would have to send for her mother and father.

And if her mother and father came to school to talk to the teacher, that would be one day her mother could not weave. One day.

On the playground, Annie's teacher was in charge of the gym class.

"Who will lead the exercises today?" she asked.

No one answered.

The teacher laughed, "Very well. Then I shall be leader." The teacher was young. Her blue skirt was wide and the heels on her brown shoes were high. The teacher kicked off her shoes, and the children laughed.

Annie followed the teacher's lead — bending, jumping, and she waited for the time when the teacher would lead them in jogging around the playground.

As Annie jogged past the spot where the teacher's shoes lay on the ground, she picked up a shoe and hid it in the folds of her dress.

When Annie jogged past a trash can, she dropped the shoe inside.

Some of the children saw her and laughed, but some frowned and were serious. When the line jogged near the schoolhouse door, Annie slipped

from the line and went inside to her room and her own desk.

Clearly she heard the teacher as she spoke to the children outside.

"The other shoe, please." Her voice was pleasant. Then there was silence.

Limping, one shoe on and one shoe gone, the teacher came into the room.

The children followed, giggling and holding their hands across their mouths.

"I know it's funny," the teacher said, "but now I need the shoe."

Annie looked at the boards of the floor. A shiny black beetle crawled between the cracks.

The door opened, and another teacher came inside with a shoe in his hand. As he passed Annie's desk, he touched her shoulder and smiled down at her.

"I saw someone playing tricks," he said.

The teacher looked at Annie, and the room was very still.

When school was over for the day, Annie waited.

Timidly, with hammering heart, she went to the teacher's desk.

"Do you want my mother and father to come to the school tomorrow?" she asked.

"No, Annie," the teacher said. "I have the shoe. Everything is all right."

Annie's face was hot, and her hands were cold. She turned and ran. She was the last to climb on the bus.

Finally, there was her own bus stop. She hopped down and slowly trudged the long way home. She stopped beside the loom.

The rug was now much higher than her waist.

That night she curled up in her blanket. She slept lightly and awakened before dawn.

There was no sound from her mother's sheepskin. Her grandmother was a quiet hump in her blanket. Annie heard only her father's loud, sleeping breathing. There was no other sound on the whole earth, except the howling of a coyote from far across the desert.

In the dim light of early morning, Annie crept outside to the night pen where the sheep were sleeping. The dry wood creaked when she undid the gate and pushed it wide open.

She tugged at the sleeping sheep until one stood quietly. Then the others stood also, uncertain — shoving together. The lead goat turned toward the open gate, and Annie slipped her fingers through his belled collar. She curled her fingertips across the bell, muffling its sound, and led the goat through the gate. The sheep followed.

She led them across the sand and around the small mesa where she released the goat.

"Go," she said.

She ran back to the hogan and slid under her blanket and lay shivering. Now her family would hunt the sheep all day. This would be the day when her mother would not weave.

When the fullness of morning came and it was light, Annie watched her grandmother rise and go outside.

Annie heard her call.

"The sheep are gone."

Annie's mother and father hurried outside, and Annie followed.

Her mother moaned softly, "The sheep — the sheep — "

"I see them," the grandmother said. "They graze near the mesa."

Annie went with her grandmother, and when they reached the sheep, Annie's fingers slipped under the goat's collar, and the bell tinkled sharply as the sheep followed back to the pen.

In school that day, Annie sat quietly and wondered what more she could do. When the teacher asked questions, Annie looked at the floor. She did not even hear.

When night came, she curled up in her blanket, but not to sleep.

When everything was still, she slipped from her blanket and crept outside.

The sky was dark and secret. The wind was soft against her face. For a moment, she stood waiting

until she could see in the night. She went to
the loom.

She felt for the weaving stick there in its place
among the warp strings. She separated the warp and
felt for the wool.

Slowly she pulled out the strands of yarn, one
by one.

One by one, she laid them across her knees.

And when the row was removed, she separated
the strings of the warp again and reached for the
second row.

When the woven rug was only as high as her
waist, she crept back to her blanket, taking the
strands of wool with her.

Under the blanket, she smoothed the strands and made them into a ball. And then she slept.

The next night, Annie removed another day's weaving. In the morning when her mother went to the loom, she looked at the weaving — puzzled.

For a moment, she pressed her fingers against her eyes.

The Old One looked at Annie curiously. Annie held her breath.

The third night, Annie crept to the loom.

A gentle hand touched her shoulder.

"Go to sleep, my granddaughter," the Old One said.

Annie wanted to throw her arms around her grandmother's waist and tell her why she had been bad, but she could only stumble to her blanket and huddle under it and let the tears roll into the edge of her hair.

When morning came, Annie unrolled herself from the blanket and helped prepare the morning meal.

Afterward, she followed her grandmother through the cornfield. Her grandmother walked slowly, and Annie fitted her steps to the slow steps of the Old One.

When they reached the small mesa, the Old One sat, crossing her knees and folding her gnarled fingers into her lap.

Annie knelt beside her.

The Old One looked far off toward the rim of desert where sky met sand.

"My granddaughter," she said, "you have tried to hold back time. This cannot be done." The desert stretched yellow and brown away to the edge of the morning sky. "The sun comes up from the edge of earth in the morning. It returns to the edge of earth in the evening. Earth, from which good things come for the living creatures on it. Earth, to which all creatures finally go."

Annie picked up a handful of brown sand and pressed it against the palm of her hand. Slowly, she let it fall to earth. She understood many things.

The sun rose but it also set.

The cactus did not bloom forever. Petals dried and fell to earth.

She knew that she was a part of the earth and the things in it. She would always be a part of the earth, just as her grandmother had always been, just as her grandmother would always be, always and forever.

And Annie was breathless with the wonder of it.

They walked back to the hogan together, Annie and the Old One.

Annie picked up the old weaving stick.

"I am ready to weave," she said to her mother.

"I will use the stick that my grandmother has given me." She knelt at the loom.

She separated the warp strings and slipped the weaving stick in place, as her mother had done, as her grandmother had done.

She picked up a strand of gray wool and started to weave.

Author

This author has written many fine children's books under her pen name, Miska Miles, and under her real name, Patricia Miles Martin. She has been a teacher as well as an author of stories and poems. *Annie and the Old One,* winner of several book awards, was a Newbery Medal Honor Book.

Comprehension Questions

1. Why didn't Annie want her mother to finish the rug?
2. When the Old One asked Annie and her parents to choose a gift, what gift did Annie choose?
3. What were some ways in which Annie tried to hold back time? Do you think she might try to hold back time again? Why or why not?

Vocabulary

The words below were used to describe how Annie and her family felt or acted at different times. Use the words to fill in the blanks in the sentences. Then complete each sentence.

puzzled   breathless   curiously   respectfully

1. Annie and her parents stood _____ as the Old One told them . . .
2. Annie's mother was _____ because . . .
3. The Old One looked at Annie _____ because . . .
4. Annie was _____ with wonder after . . .

Writing an Interview

Pretend that you are a newspaper reporter interviewing Annie about her family and life on the mesa. Write your questions and Annie's answers.

My Grandmother Tells Me

by Ann Nolan Clark

My grandmother tells me,
  "For two summer moons
  I will walk with you
  across the sand patches,
  by the rock ridges
  and the cacti,
  through the dry washes
  and along the sandy trails
  that you may know the desert
  and hold its beauty
  in your heart forever."

Sensory Images

Read the riddle below.

What am I?
Large and powerful
with a huge hairy head,
small eyes, small ears,
a den holds my bed.
A shaggy coat,
a good sense of smell,
over the hills I come
on four strong legs.

The animal in the riddle is a bear. The words *shaggy* and *hairy* help you to picture what a bear looks like. The words *hairy head* describe an animal that has a lot of hair on its head. The words *shaggy coat* tell you that the animal has long, thick fur all over its body.

You don't have to speak in riddles to tell what something looks like. You can use picture words, such as *shaggy* and *hairy,* that help others see in their minds what you are describing or talking about. Authors use many picture words when they write so that readers can have a clear image, or picture, of what they read.

Read the paragraphs on page 279. As you read, try to picture in your mind the things that are being described.

Then draw a picture for one of the paragraphs. Share your picture with the class. Tell which words in the paragraph helped you to "see" the picture that you drew.

The Tarantula

The sun comes up over the mesa. The desert starts to wake. Wild flowers open their faces to the new day. An early bee sings to the yellow poppy. From under a rock, a tarantula steps out of hiding. This large hairy spider moves over the sand, silent and slow. It is looking for food.

The sun climbs up and up. The purple sky is streaked with blue and orange, like the colors on a loom. Above the coppery-red bluffs, a hawk rides on a stream of air. Down below, a mouse scurries and skips into a hole.

The spider does not see the sky; the sky is too big. It does not see the hawk; the hawk is too high. It does not see the mouse; the mouse is too quick. It sees only what is small, and near, and slow. The spider sees a butterfly resting on a finger of grass. Its petal-like wings open and close, but it does not fly away.

Predicting Outcomes

When you read a story, you are given certain information by the author. You also have information of your own that you knew before you started to read. As you read, you can put together the information the author gives you and things you already know to figure out what will happen next in the story, what a character will do, or how the story will end. It is interesting to see if you can guess what will happen before the author tells you.

By using the information in a story and what you already know to figure out what will happen next, you will become a better reader because you are "getting into the story." You are involved. This will help you to understand the story better and enjoy it more.

When you decide in advance what is about to happen in a story or situation, you are predicting an outcome. To predict an outcome you should (1) use the information — facts and ideas — given by the author, and (2) use the things you already know from your own experience.

When the grandmother said on page 263 of "Annie and the Old One," "My children, when the new rug is taken from the loom, I will go to Mother Earth," you predicted that she was probably going to die soon. The facts given in the story that supported that prediction are listed below.

1. The grandmother was very old.
2. Annie's mother had tears in her eyes.
3. The grandmother asked each family member to choose a gift.

Sometimes you have to change your prediction as you read more of the story. In "Annie and the Old One," new information was not added. The more you read, the more your first prediction, about the probable death of the grandmother, proved correct.

Read the paragraph below and see if you can predict what is going to happen.

Roger and his brother, Bobby, liked to play tricks on each other. One hot summer day, their dad asked Roger to hook up the hose and water the grass. Just as Roger was about to turn on the water, Bobby came out of the house. Roger looked at his brother and smiled. "This will be great fun," he said to himself.

---

1. What do you think Roger is going to do?
2. What information in the story makes you think that?

The writer knew you would know what a hose is, and how people sometimes play tricks on others when using a hose on a hot day. Writers expect readers to use their knowledge if that knowledge is something that most people will know.

Suppose the author went on to write: *Roger began to laugh as Bobby ran into the house, a little wet from the hose.*

3. What do you think Bobby is going to do?

Suppose the author continued to write: *When Bobby went into the house, he opened a closet and got out a raincoat and boots.*

4. Is that what you thought Bobby was going to do? Did you have to change your original prediction?

Sometimes as an author adds information, you may change a prediction you have made.

It is important that readers have as much knowledge as possible and then use it together with the information that is given to predict an outcome. You can get that knowledge from parents, teachers, and friends. Traveling, movies, television, and pictures also help you gain knowledge.

You are being taught how to read so that on your own you can read to learn many things. You can learn many things by being a good listener also.

Predicting an Outcome

Read the paragraphs below. Use the information you are given and knowledge from your own experience to answer the questions that follow the paragraphs.

The guests arrived at 2:00 P.M. Everyone brought something to eat or drink. Some people brought sausages and rolls, spare ribs, or hamburgers. Others brought fruit juices. Lori led the guests to the back yard where her father had set up the grill.

Everyone was having a wonderful time when there was a sudden loud roll of thunder and the sky became dark.

"Oh, no!" shouted Lori. "Why must that happen now?"

---

1. What do you think is taking place in Lori's back yard?
2. What information in the paragraph makes you think that?
3. What do the loud roll of thunder and the dark sky tell you is about to happen?
4. What do you think Lori and the guests will do now that the sky has turned dark and there has been a loud roll of thunder? What makes you think that?

Skill Summary

- When you read a story, you can use the information the author gives and knowledge from your own experience to predict an outcome.

- You may have to change your prediction as you read more of a story and get new information.

- You can get the knowledge you bring to your reading from parents, teachers, friends, traveling, movies, television, pictures, and from other things you read. It is important to be a good reader and a good listener.

The Mail-Order Monster

by Sheila Gordon

To: Julius Graham
38 E. Third Street
Tulsa, Oklahoma

Acme Novelty Company
307 N. Fulton Street
Fresno, California
93721

A monster that walks and talks — for only $4.99! Will Julius's mail-order monster be everything he hopes it will be?

When Julius saw the ad for a monster, he knew that he wanted one. He didn't know how much a really good monster should cost, but the price sounded right. So Julius earned the money and sent off his order.

Months went by, and the letter carrier still hadn't delivered his monster. Julius began to worry. Would it fit into the mailbox? Or would it be delivered in an enormous truck? Maybe his monster wouldn't arrive at all!

Just when Julius had almost lost hope, a package arrived. . . .

Julius came home from school and ran into his bedroom to get his baseball bat. There, lying in the middle of his bed, was a small package.

He picked it up and saw his name and address on the label. It came from the Acme Novelty Company in Fresno, California. It was wrapped in brown paper and tied up with string.

He held the package in the palm of his hand. It did not feel very heavy. In fact, it felt rather light.

He took it to show his mother, who was busy working on a drawing of the webbed toes of the Javanese flying frog. His mother was an illustrator for scientific journals. She had her drawing board set up in the study and did drawings of whales or worms, or bones or stones, or mushrooms or minnows, or whatever the scientists needed to illustrate what they wrote about.

"What's this?" Julius asked, showing his mother the package. "It was on my bed."

"Well, it came for you in the mail this morning," she said.

"Hmm, I wonder what it could be," Julius said. "I *was* expecting a monster, but this couldn't be it. A monster couldn't fit into a box as small as this . . . could it?" he asked his mother.

"I'm not sure, really, honey. Why not open it and see what it is," his mother said.

So Julius took his mother's scissors and cut the string. Then he unwrapped the brown wrapping paper and opened up the stiff cardboard box. He took out of the box a flippy-flappy, rolled-up, rubbery-flubbery, red thing, and unrolled it, and spread it out on the floor.

He and his mother both looked at it. It was made of thick red rubber and had big yellow dots all over it.

It had a face painted on one end, a tie and six buttons in the middle, and two shoes painted on the other end. It didn't look like a monster at all.

It lay flat on the floor, looking up at Julius and his mother. Julius and his mother looked down at it. Then they looked at each other.

"It's my *monster!*" Julius cried in disappointment.

His mother also looked rather sad about the monster. "Well, now," she said, "let's take a look at it, anyway. I think it's supposed to be blown up."

So they went to look for Buffy, Julius's brother, to ask him to pump it up with his bicycle pump.

"What *is* it?" Buffy wanted to know.

"It's my monster," Julius said.

"Well," Buffy said, "let's pump it up and see what's supposed to happen."

So they took turns at pumping up the monster. Lizzie, Julius's sister, came along to see what it was all about, and so did George, their dog.

The monster puffed up and grew bigger and bigger. When it was all filled up with air, they stopped pumping.

Then Julius stood it up and said to everyone, "Shh . . . shh . . . wait."

When George came sniffing around the monster's feet to check if it was a friend or an enemy, Julius said, "*Stop* that, George! *Shh*, everyone . . . wait . . . quiet. . . ."

"What are we waiting *for*?" Lizzie asked.

"Shh . . . it's supposed to walk and talk," Julius told her. "It's a walking and talking monster."

Julius's mother and Lizzie and Buffy all looked at each other, but they didn't say anything. They all waited, but the monster didn't talk.

It didn't walk, either. It just slowly toppled over and lay on its side on the floor.

Buffy picked up the monster and punched it down and said, "You old monster — why won't you walk or talk? A fine walking and talking monster *you've* turned out to be!" The monster bounced about and fell over and bounced up again.

George began to chase the monster and yap excitedly and snap at its feet, and Julius began to laugh. They all romped about, wrestling with the monster and shouting and bouncing it around the room — when suddenly — there was a very loud BANG!

George ran away and hid behind the sofa. There on the floor lay a large flat piece of torn red rubber — and no more monster.

George came out from behind the sofa and whined.

Buffy said, "What a terrible old monster *that* turned out to be."

Lizzie said, "Oh, well. . . ." They all stood about looking at the exploded monster, and George went and sniffed suspiciously at it.

After a while, Lizzie said, "Julius, would you like to try my new mosaic tile set?" It was very kind of her as she had just gotten it for her birthday and hadn't used it herself yet.

However, Julius was very mad now, and he yelled, "It didn't even WALK, and it didn't TALK. It wasn't FORTY-EIGHT INCHES TALL EITHER!"

His mother said, "I'm sorry, dear — it's a big disappointment, I know."

Lizzie said, "Let's go, Julius. You can tile a dish if you like."

So Julius went to Lizzie's room, and she showed him how to fit all the little colored tiles with cement and grout to make a dish.

Their mother said to Buffy, "Better put this poor old monster outside in the trash, Buffy. Julius will get upset all over again if he sees it lying around."

So that was the end of the monster.

Julius was very quiet for the rest of the afternoon and the evening. His father came home and they had dinner. After dinner they all ate some cherries that their mother served in the dish that Julius had made. Julius was very quiet.

Then he did his homework. He took a bath and brushed his teeth. He said good night to his family and went to bed.

In the middle of the night, Julius's mother woke up. She lay awake in the dark wondering what had woken her. Then she heard a strange sound.

Tik tik tik-tik-tik tik.

She woke Julius's father. "Can you hear a strange sound?" she asked him.

Tik-tik tik tik tik-tik-tik-tik-tik.

"I wonder what it is," he said.

So they both got out of bed and followed the strange sound until they came to the study.

The light was on in the study.

Tik tik tik-tik-tik tik.

Julius was sitting at the desk in the study, in his pajamas, typing.

"Julius!" his mother said. "What on earth are you doing? It's way past midnight!"

"I'm writing a letter," Julius said.

"To whom?" his mother and father asked together.

"To the monster people," Julius said.

"Can't it wait till morning?" his mother asked.

"No!" Julius said.

"Well," his mother said, "we're going back to bed. Make sure you turn off the lights when you're through writing that letter, Julius."

The next day was Saturday, and at breakfast Julius showed them all his monster letter.

It went like this:

Dear Sir,
    Yesterday I received a monster. There
were a few things wrong with it. It was
not 48 inches tall. It did not talk—or walk.
And it popped a few minutes after I got it.
    I would like my money back.

                                    From,
                                    Julius

His mother and father looked at each other across the breakfast table, and they both said they thought it was a good letter.

After breakfast Buffy and Julius put George on the leash and went off to mail the letter.

In a dusty little office in a warehouse in Fresno, California, a secretary named Iris was sitting at her desk. All around her, from the floor to the ceiling, were shelves filled with cardboard cartons. The cartons were all labeled. There were labels like:

Rubber Masks
(with hair — savage monster, fierce gorilla,
horrible Frankenstein, $2.99)

Monster Record
(eerie groans, terrifying thunderstorms,
screams, hideous laughter, many more, $1.89)

Lifelike Mouse
(crawls, creeps up sleeve;
scare your friends, $1.39)

There was a knock at the door, and the letter carrier came in with a bundle of letters.

Iris opened the letters, put them in a wire basket, and took them to another office.

"Mail's here, Fred," she said.

Fred looked through the pile of mail. Then he said, "Kid here wants his money back. Send him the regular reply."

A few days later, Julius received a letter from the Acme Novelty Company, Fresno, California.

It said:

Dear Sir/Madam:
    As you are not satisfied with the goods you received, you may order anything else from our catalog to the value of $5.00. A catalog is enclosed.

Yours truly,
Acme Novelty Company

Julius showed the letter and the catalog to Buffy and Lizzie.

"Wow — five dollars," Buffy said.

"Let's see what else you could get," Lizzie said. "How about a magnet that lifts fifty pounds of solid steel?"

"Or a bargain bag of popular tricks?" Buffy said.

"Or a pocket spy telescope?" suggested Lizzie.

Buffy and Lizzie were reading from the catalog with such interest that neither of them noticed that Julius was getting upset. Suddenly he yelled, "I DON'T WANT ANYTHING FROM THEIR OLD CATALOG! I ONLY WANT MY MONEY BACK! They said in the advertisement, 'Satisfaction guaranteed or your money refunded,' AND I'M NOT SATISIFIED ONE BIT WITH THEIR MONSTER!"

"Why not write and tell them?" Lizzie suggested.

So Julius sat down at the typewriter.

> Dear Sir,
>   I am not satisfied with that monster. I don't want anything else. I would like my money back.
>
>   From,
>   Julius

Back in the dusty office in Fresno, California, Iris opened the letter from Julius and took it in to Fred.

"Kid just wants his money back, Fred," she said.

Fred put out his hand for the letter, read it, and shrugged his shoulders.

"So send it to him," he said.

So Julius received a check for four dollars and ninety-nine cents. He showed it to his mother, and she changed it into a five dollar bill for him. "Keep the change," she said.

Then Julius and Buffy and Lizzie and George all went off to the stores.

"Where are you four going?" their mother called out the window.

"We're going with Julius to spend his monster money — we're going to try the bookstore first," Lizzie answered.

The old bookstore was their favorite store. An old sign above the window said:

BOOKS: BOUGHT AND SOLD
USED — SECONDHAND
RARE — OUT OF PRINT

The store was filled with old books that crowded the shelves and stood piled on tables and overflowed from boxes onto the floor.

There was a smell of books and dust and old yellowing papers. The bookseller didn't mind how long they spent browsing through the piles of books, just as long as they put them back in the right place after they had looked at them.

Julius and Buffy and Lizzie sat down on some old wooden crates. It was nice and warm and dusty sitting on a crate and leafing through old books.

"If I were you, I'd get this book," Buffy said. "It's all about how there's an ice age due in ten thousand years."

"How many years?" Julius asked.

"Ten thousand."

"Ten *thousand!* Whew! You had me worried for a moment," Julius said.

The bookseller came by, balancing a pile of books that reached up as high as his forehead. "Having a good time, kids?" his voice came out from behind the books.

"Yes," they all said.

"Put the books back just where you took them from," he said, and he disappeared behind some bookshelves.

"Maybe I should get this," Julius said.

He showed them a thin yellow book called *How to Play the French Horn in Ten Easy Lessons*. Buffy and

Lizzie just looked at him as if to say "What next?" So he put it back just where he had taken it from.

"You should get this book about wolves," Lizzie said. "It looks really good. It says here that wolves aren't fierce animals at all — they're actually very kind and don't attack human beings as is commonly believed."

"You should get this book about insects," Buffy said. "The pictures are really neat."

Julius said, "I'm having a hard time making up my mind."

"Take your time," the bookseller's wife said. "We stay open till seven tonight."

At last they chose a book. Julius went over to the counter carrying under his arm a big old book with a red leather cover and gold lettering. It was called *The Monster Book of Fairy Tales*. The pages were of heavy paper, and each story had a brightly colored picture page. There were pictures of castles and dragons and giants and forests with trees shaped like monsters, and even the clouds in the skies were strange and eerie shapes.

They all agreed that it was the book to buy, but they thought it would cost more than five dollars.

"How much is this book of fairy tales?" Julius asked the bookseller.

"This is quite a valuable old book," he said, looking through it.

Julius felt quite worried, as he very much wanted to have it. "Is it more than five dollars?" Julius asked.

"Well," said the man thoughtfully, "by a strange coincidence, this book costs exactly five dollars — including tax."

"Whew," Julius said, "you had me worried for a moment."

When they got home, Julius went straight to his room and lay down on his stomach on the bed and opened his book of fairy tales.

The first story he read was about a boy no bigger than your thumb, who saves his whole family from a wicked ogre.

Then Lizzie popped her head around the door and said, "Julius, dinner's nearly ready."

"Coming," Julius answered, but he turned over the page and kept reading until Buffy came into the room and said, "How's that book?"

Julius said, "It's great — look at this picture."

They both looked at a picture of an ugly wolf with red eyes and long, fanged teeth.

"Scary, isn't it?" Julius said.

"Mm-hmm," Buffy agreed, "but you must come and eat now."

"I'll be right there," Julius said, without even looking up from the book. He read until his father came into the room and said, "Julius! Dinner is on the table, and you haven't even washed your hands yet."

"I'll·be right there, Dad, but just take a look at this book I bought with the monster money."

His father sat down on the bed beside him. Julius showed him the pictures of glass mountains and golden roads. They were both looking at a picture of

an elf who could change straw into gold, when the door opened and Julius's mother walked in.

"What's going on here?" she asked. "Dinner's getting cold."

"Sorry," his father said. "It's this book that Julius bought with his monster money — have you seen it?"

"I'll look at it *after* dinner," his mother said. "I've spent all afternoon drawing diagrams of the way beavers build dams, with hundreds and hundreds of small twigs and branches. So right now, the only thing that really interests me is a plate of steaming lamb stew."

"We'll be right there," his father said. "Julius, go and wash your hands."

At last they all sat down to dinner.

"Julius, don't gobble your food like that," his father said.

"What's the rush?" his mother asked.

"Well, I want to get back to my book," Julius said.

"There's this story I want to read about a dragon all covered with shiny green scales. When he breathes, streams of fire and smoke come pouring out of his nostrils and his eyes blaze and whole forests and villages burn down. . . ."

"Sounds better than a red rubber mail-order monster that pops after you've had it about five minutes," Buffy said.

"Oh," Julius said, and he started to eat his spinach more slowly, "it is — much better!"

Author

Sheila Gordon is the author of *A Monster in the Mailbox*, part of which you have just read. She wrote the story because she remembered how very disappointed her eight-year-old son was with what he got from a mail-order company. He had hoped to have a "real, live" monster, just as Julius did in the story.

Thinking It Over

Comprehension Questions

1. What did the mail-order monster turn out to be?

2. What made Julius's mother wake up in the middle of the night?

3. How do you think Fred might have felt when he read Julius's letter?

4. Would you have ordered something else from the monster catalog to take the place of the monster that popped? Why or why not?

5. What did Julius get from reading his monster book that he did not get from his monster?

Vocabulary

The words in the box are from the story. Use them in sentences to describe a monster.

enormous	**eerie**	**fierce**
strange	**hideous**	**terrifying**

Writing Paragraphs

Make a book cover for *The Monster Book of Fairy Tales* that Julius bought. Write something about the kinds of stories that were in the book to put on the inside of the cover.

Flip-Flop Words

Roly-poly, *rubbery-flubbery*, and *flippy-flappy* are flip-flop words. Flip-flop words tell how things look, feel, or sound. The flip-flop word *roly-poly* describes something short and plump. *Rubbery-flubbery* describes how something made out of rubber might feel. *Flippy-flappy* describes the sound of something made of rubber before it is filled with air.

Splish-splash is an example of a flip-flop word that describes how something sounds. *Splish-splash* is the sound the water makes when someone plays in the swimming pool.

Match the flip-flop words below with what you think they describe.

fuzzy-wuzzy	horse
ding-dong	magic
clip-clop	rain
pitter-patter	bell
itty-bitty	bear
razzle-dazzle	ant

Now try making up some of your own flip-flop words. Use these beginnings. Then tell what they might describe.

teeny-	**wiggly-**
willy-	**snip-**

Uncle Somebody and Becky's Birthday

by Virginia Hamilton

Becky's uncle and his family travel from Seattle, Washington to Ohio to celebrate Becky's birthday. What do they travel in? What special birthday present does Becky receive from her uncle?

"I don't believe Uncle Somebody is coming at all," Becky Stewart said glumly. "Whoever heard of anyone coming all the way from Seattle, Washington to Ohio by covered wagon!"

"And it's the 1980's too!" said her mother, laughing as she prepared dinner.

"Are you laughing at me?" asked Becky.

"I'm just teasing you, honey," her mother said fondly. "You know your Uncle Lewis has a lot of fun with kids. That's the reason he likes you children to call him Uncle Somebody. And that's why he wrote to you, telling you that all of them would be here on Saturday to celebrate your eighth birthday."

It was a fine August evening in Ohio. Becky and her four-year-old brother, Larry, sat at the round kitchen table. Uncle Somebody's letter lay open on the table. Becky had just read it for the third time.

"Just look at that sunset!" exclaimed their mother, peering out of the screen door. Both Becky and Larry looked around to see the last sunrays going down, tinging everything orange and red. The Stewarts lived at the edge of town, where they could view the peaceful country fields.

"Do you think Uncle Somebody's seeing that sunset?" asked Becky.

"I suppose he is," said her mother, smiling to herself. "Oh, it will be so good to see him. I haven't seen Lewis for so long!"

"I've *never* seen him," said Larry, "but I know why he's called 'Uncle Somebody.'"

"Why?" asked Becky, eyeing her brother.

Larry pouted. "I can't remember all of it," he said finally.

Becky grinned and said, "I know! It's because he was named after all of his daddy's best friends."

"That's right," said her mother. "My father, your Grandpa Jones, named Lewis after every one of his closest friends."

"Uncle Somebody's real, whole name," said Becky, taking a deep breath, "is . . . *Lewis, Augustus, Leopold, Dr. Williams, John Applegate Jones!*"

"That's it," said her mother, her eyes shining with memories. "When your Grandpa Morris Jones wanted Lewis for something, he would call: 'Come on home, Lewis, Augustus, Leopold, Dr. Williams, John Applegate Jones. Come on ho-ome!'"

"That's really something," said Becky.

"Lewis, Augus-tus, Leo-pold, Dr. Will . . ." Larry said, attempting to say his uncle's whole name. He couldn't finish it. "I'd rather call him Uncle Somebody," he sighed.

"So would everybody else," agreed Becky. "With a name like that, you really *are* somebody."

"*Uncle* Somebody," said Larry. "And he's coming just to see us too."

"To see *me*," Becky said, "on my birthday!"

"Now, Becky," said her mother, "Lewis is coming to visit everyone. Your birthday party will be for everyone to share."

Becky pouted. "I know that," she said, eyeing her little brother. It was hard not to want Uncle Somebody all to herself. "It's getting exciting!" she said. "I can hardly wait!"

Becky's mother had already started baking bread and freezing it for the company. Uncle Somebody and his family would be staying a week. Becky's father baked wonderful cakes, but he wouldn't do that until probably Friday night. Her father worked the whole year round, but her mother was a teacher and was home for the summer.

After visiting at Becky's house, Uncle Somebody and his family would travel to the famous Niagara Falls, way up by Buffalo, New York. Becky couldn't imagine it. Just the name thrilled her — Niagara Falls!

"I hope Uncle Somebody doesn't waste a lot of time," Becky said anxiously. "Here it is Tuesday already, and he's not even here."

"Lewis has the whole week to get here," her mother said.

"But I don't see how it's possible for Uncle Somebody to arrive here by Saturday if he's driving a *covered wagon*," Becky said.

Her mother smiled but wouldn't tell whether she knew the answer.

"I wish it was my birthday," Larry said, with the saddest expression on his face.

"You just had your birthday," Becky said. "It was June the second. Don't you remember anything?"

Larry looked hurt. His face seemed to break up in
pieces.

"It's *my* birthday," Becky yelled. "Even if you cry,
you can't have it!"

"Becky, hush!" said her mother sternly. "Stop
making him cry."

"I didn't make him cry," protested Becky. "He just
cries for nothing! It's *my* birthday, and Uncle Somebody is coming to see *me*."

"You won't have a good time Saturday if you keep
on being persnickety," said her mother.

Tears were in Larry's eyes, but he had stopped
crying. "What's per . . . persni . . . , what you said?"
he asked his mother.

"It's what you are all the time — a pest!" Becky
said impatiently.

"Keep it up," said her mother in a warning voice. She took Becky by the arm and pointed her toward her room. Becky rushed upstairs into her room and flung herself on her bed, just about as mad as a hornet. She was afraid something terrible would happen to spoil her birthday.

That night, as she went to get a drink of water, Becky heard her parents' voices coming from the living room.

She heard her mother say to her dad, "Becky's been out of sorts all day. Lewis has her all excited and upset. You know his letter said they were coming in a 'covered wagon.' "

Both her mother and father chuckled.

"What in the world is so funny about a covered wagon?" Becky wondered.

"I'll go up and have a word with her," her father said, putting his newspaper down.

Becky heard him start across the living room. She raced on tip-toe back to her room. When her father came in, she was scrunched down under the sheet, her nose in her storybook.

"Hi, Daddy," she said, as casually as she could. She yawned deeply.

"I'm glad I caught you before you went to dreamland with the light on," her father said, smoothing her hair. "I hear you were upset with your brother today."

"I was not," Becky said.

"Your mother said you were," he said gently, and sat down beside her.

"Well, Mama got it all wrong," she said, sticking out her chin. "Larry wanted my *birthday*."

"Becky, he's just a little boy who thinks every day should be a party," her father said.

She looked up at her father and took his big, familiar hand in hers.

"Daddy, I'm just so excited about Saturday."

"I know you are, Becky, but don't let it get out of hand. Larry is just as excited as you are."

"Okay, I won't, anymore," she said, and she really meant it.

"That's my girl," her father said.

"I don't suppose you can tell me what kind of covered wagon Uncle Somebody is coming in and how many horses are pulling it, can you, Daddy?"

"No, I don't suppose I can," he said. "You'll just have to wait and see."

"I'll never make it," she sighed. That made him smile.

Her father patted her cheek and planted a kiss on her forehead. He took the book and placed it on the table beside her bed.

"Sleep tight," he told her, as he turned off the lamp.

In minutes, Becky was asleep. She slept fitfully, though, all through the night. In the morning, she woke up feeling tired and worse than ever.

Wednesday and Thursday seemed to Becky to go by very slowly; however, she managed to get through them. On Friday she spent half the day in her room. Then she sniffed what smelled like cake baking. The aroma was irresistible.

"Daddy!" she yelled.

"Come on down!" he yelled back.

Downstairs, Becky found her mother and father in the kitchen. Her mom was making sandwiches for lunch. Becky was just in time. Her dad was baking a cake.

"My birthday cake?" she asked.

"Yes," he said, "two layers and extra sheet cakes with pink icing too."

"Boy, I guess you needed to come home early to get all that done," Becky said.

"I sure did," he agreed.

They ate egg salad sandwiches in the kitchen with the good cake aroma surrounding them. Becky leaned on her father's shoulder. He didn't mind.

"I love summer," she murmured, "and I love birthdays and relatives."

Nothing could stop Saturday from coming. At last Becky realized that. She helped her mom and dad all afternoon. Now it was Friday night, and supper was over. Larry had fallen asleep on the couch, and their dad had carried him up to bed. Becky was feeling a little sleepy, too, so she went up to her room.

She put on her pajamas and climbed into bed. "Bet I don't sleep a wink," she thought. "I'm so tired, and I'm so nervous. If Uncle Somebody isn't here in the morning, I don't know what I'll do."

Her mother came to kiss her goodnight and pull the sheet up, but Becky was out like a light.

Becky woke up with a start. All was dark, so she turned over, thought of nothing, and slept. The next time she woke up, it was still dark. Someone had closed her curtains.

"My!" Becky cried. She could see the sun shining. "Where did the night go so fast? Oh! Oh, happy birthday to me . . . it's today!" she thought.

She got up and tip-toed to her parents' bedroom, but they were not there. "Don't start without me!" Becky thought. Her brother was still fast asleep in his bedroom.

Becky went into the bathroom. She washed her face, brushed her teeth, and combed her curly hair. The dress she put on was a yellow sun-dress — nice for company who were relatives. She went downstairs, but there was nobody in the living room and no one in the kitchen. Becky noticed her birthday

cake on top of the refrigerator. It was wonderful-looking, gleaming with pink icing.

She went back through the house and opened the front door, stepping out onto the porch. Her dad's blue sedan was in the driveway. She walked out to the mailbox, but there wasn't any covered wagon parked at the curb. Becky's heart sank.

"Where did he tie up the horses?" she wondered. With a sick feeling, she went back inside. "Where did Mama and Daddy go?" She couldn't yell, for fear she would wake her brother.

"Uncle Somebody may not come, but it's still my birthday," she thought.

Becky opened the kitchen door and went outside again.

"SURPRISE! SURPRISE!" A whole bunch of people were shouting something at her. It scared her out of her wits. A big boy leaped from a tree and another came from behind bushes. Two girls and a little boy came at her from under the clothesline.

"SURPRISE, BECKY!" everyone shouted. Now she understood.

Becky gaped at them all. It was Uncle Somebody, Aunt Maggie, and their five kids. A long green station wagon was parked beneath the huge maple tree across from the back porch. The station wagon had signs on the bumpers. "Becky's Birthday!" one read. "This is a Covered Wagon," read another.

"A station wagon!" cried Becky. "Oh, you all! A covered station wagon!"

All the kids circling her laughed. She didn't mind at all. She couldn't get over the sign that read, "Becky's Birthday!" It had come all the way from Seattle.

"The whole world knows my name!" she thought.

She ran under the tree. Uncle Somebody was standing there in front of the station wagon with her mother and father and Aunt Maggie. She had been so excited, she hadn't seen them for the maple.

He was not as tall as her father. He had a cap on his head and a blue kerchief tied around his neck. His eyes were dark and full of laughter.

"Uncle Somebody," she whispered.

319

"Becky Stewart! My, how you've grown!" Uncle Somebody said. He swung her up, gave her a big hug, and stood her on her feet again.

After that, everything happened so fast. All the kids came around. Becky remembered their names and soon could put a name to a familiar face. Aunt Maggie had her arm around Becky.

Everybody had breakfast, with raucous noise and laughter in the dining room. Larry woke up. Her mother brought him down to meet everybody.

Becky found out during the day that Uncle Somebody's "horses" meant the horsepower of his station wagon, which had to do with the power of the car's engine.

"Horses — another joke!" she told Uncle Somebody. She was leaning on his shoulder, the way she would lean on her father's shoulder.

"I bet you can't guess what's *not* a joke," Uncle Somebody said.

"What's that?" Becky asked.

"That you are going to Niagara Falls with us next Saturday," Uncle Somebody said, winking at her.

"What?" Becky said in amazement. "Niagara Falls — me?"

"Only if you want to go with us. You surely can," said Uncle Somebody. "Happy Birthday, Becky!"

"Oh, wow! I want to go, I do!" Becky exclaimed.

Everybody had a grand old time at Becky's birthday celebration. She blew out all of the candles in one breath. She got games from her cousins. Aunt

Maggie made her the prettiest yellow knit-and-purled sweater dress she had ever seen. Her mom and dad and Larry gave her playclothes and a new storybook.

Seeing the famous Niagara Falls was the best present of all. It was a sight to remember, to tell her class at school. How she and her cousins drove all the way to Buffalo, New York, in Uncle *Somebody's* green covered wagon — pulled by horses too!

Author

Virginia Hamilton has received every major award and honor given to American authors of children's books. Her books are mostly for older readers, but one that you might enjoy reading is *Jahdu*. Ms. Hamilton says that her greatest pleasure is sitting down and weaving a tale out of her past and present.

Thinking It Over

Comprehension Questions

1. What did Uncle Somebody and his family travel in to get to Ohio? What special birthday gift did Becky receive from her uncle?
2. What was unusual about Uncle Somebody's real name?

322

3. In the story, Becky called Larry a pest. Do you think he was really a pest? Why or why not?
4. What do you think Becky will tell her class about her special birthday gift?

Vocabulary

Make up clues about the words in the box. Use the Glossary if you are unsure of the meaning of a word. Ask a friend to guess which word you are thinking of.

bumpers	**couch**	**relatives**
hornet	**kerchief**	**expression**

Use each word in a sentence.

Writing Paragraphs

Becky's birthday was special because her relatives drove from Seattle, Washington to Ohio to be with her on that day. She also received a most unusual birthday gift. Write about a very special birthday you have had or about a birthday that you helped to make special for someone else.

Main Idea

You have learned that in a paragraph that is written to give you information, all of the sentences tell about one thing if the paragraph is well written. You know that the one thing all the sentences tell about is called the **topic.**

You also know that the **main idea** of a paragraph is a sentence that sums up what all the sentences are telling about the topic.

You know that a sentence that tells the main idea can be at the beginning, in the middle, or at the end of a paragraph. Sometimes paragraphs do not have a sentence that tells the main idea. Then *you* will have to figure out what the main idea is.

Read the paragraph below. The topic of the paragraph is: *How corn grows.*

In the spring of the year, a corn plant begins as a single, golden seed underground. After a while, the seed shoots up a single green leaf. Before long there are many leaves that are growing out of the center of the plant. By the middle of summer tiny ears of corn begin to form on the corn plant. Then the ears of corn become larger in size. In the fall, the dark green corn plant begins to turn brown.

Is there one sentence in the paragraph that sums up the most important — or main — idea about the topic: *How corn grows?*

Each sentence in the paragraph tells a different thing about how corn grows, but each sentence seems about as important as the others. This means that the author did not include a sentence in this paragraph that tells the main idea. Whenever this happens, you must decide the main idea yourself.

To figure out the main idea of the paragraph you need to think about the information that each of the sentences tells about the topic: *How corn grows.* You might think about each sentence as follows:

Sentence 1: how corn looks as a seed
Sentence 2: how corn looks as a tiny plant
Sentence 3: how corn looks as it gets bigger
Sentence 4: how ears of corn form on the plant
Sentence 5: how ears of corn look as they grow
Sentence 6: how the corn plant looks in the fall

All of the sentences tell about a different way that corn plants can look or how their appearance changes as they grow. If you put this information together, you can figure out the main idea of the paragraph. The main idea is: *Corn plants change in the way they look as they grow.*

Determining a Main Idea

Read the paragraph on this page. The topic of this paragraph is: *How camels look.* The paragraph does not have a sentence which tells the main idea. Use what you've learned to figure out the main idea of this paragraph. Think about what each of the sentences is telling you about the topic: *How camels look.*

Camels have faces that look too small for their bodies. Their necks are so long they have a curve in them. Camels have thick, rough lips that give them a silly look. The fur that covers the body of a camel is long and shaggy and looks as if it needs to be combed.

What did you decide was the main idea? Did you decide that *The camel is a funny-looking animal* was the main idea? Other good main idea sentences are possible. Be ready to tell yours and to tell *why* it is a good one.

You have learned that not all paragraphs that are written to give you information have sentences that tell the main idea. Sometimes *you* need to figure out the main idea of a paragraph by thinking about what the information in each of the sentences tells about the topic of the paragraph. Then you try to think of a sentence that sums up what all the sentences are telling about the topic. That sentence is the main idea.

Skill Summary

- Authors often put the main idea of a paragraph in a sentence that comes at the beginning, in the middle, or at the end of the paragraph.
- Sometimes authors do not include in a paragraph a sentence that tells the main idea, and you have to decide the main idea yourself.
- To figure out the main idea of a paragraph, think about the information the sentences tell about the topic, and then form a sentence that sums up the most important information in the sentences.

WONDERS of RIVERS

by Rae Bains

Have you ever wondered where a river begins or why there are so many rivers? Rivers are a powerful force on our planet. Find out how rivers change the land as they make their way to the sea.

Just about anywhere you live, there is a river nearby. Rivers flow past small towns and big cities. Rivers run down mountains. Rivers flow to the ocean. Rivers run through forests. Even in the desert, there are rivers.

Some rivers are very short, while others are thousands of miles long. The longest river in the United States is the Mississippi River, which is almost 2,350 miles long.

Rivers can be almost as straight as an arrow, or they can curve like a snake twisting through the grass.

Some rivers are very narrow; others are so wide that a person standing on one side cannot see someone standing on the opposite side. The Amazon River, in South America, is 90 miles wide in some places.

There are rivers that begin as tiny trickles of water from a lake. Other rivers begin as water bubbling up from under the ground.

Most rivers start as rain or snow that falls on mountains and hills.

Winter snow covers the mountaintops. In spring, the snow melts slowly. The water starts to trickle down the mountainside, forming tiny streams.

Soon, many tiny streams join together to make bigger streams that run down the sides of the mountain. The tiny streams are like the smallest branches of a tree. Where they join together, they are like the big branches of a tree. Where all the streams unite, they are like the trunk of a tree. This is the river.

Spring storms add rain to the streams of melted snow. The streams bubble as they swirl down the mountainside and tumble over the edges of large rocks.

The swift-flowing river breaks little pieces off the rocks in its path. The water pushes hard against the soil on both sides of the river, loosening sand and stones and plants. Rock, sand, and plants — everything that falls into the moving river — are swept down the mountain.

Most rivers do not move as swiftly as they seem to be moving. They travel between one to five miles an hour. You probably can pedal a bicycle faster than that.

Even when a river moves slowly, it never stops. As it moves, it wears away the ground under it and on both sides of it. Over the years, a river can wear away miles and miles of land. This wearing away of land is called *erosion*.

When a river erodes the land, it makes a groove in the ground that is shaped like the letter *V*. This V-shaped groove is called a *river valley*.

The river makes the valley deeper. Wind and rain wear away the banks of the river. After many, many years, the valley is not a V anymore. It looks more like a wide, flat *U*. In time, erosion changes a deep, narrow valley into flat land.

Where land is flat, water flows very slowly, but it never stops. There is more water coming down the mountainside, pushing at the water ahead of it. The river grows wider and longer as it moves over the land.

When water moves very slowly, it does not carry the bits of rock, sand, and plants from the mountain. These things, called *sediment,* fall to the bottom of the river. If a lot of sediment falls to the same part of the riverbed, a new piece of land will be built up. It will become an island.

Sometimes a river flows into a place where the land is very low. This low land is called a *basin*. When the river water fills the basin, it creates a lake.

Some rivers carry most of the rock and sand and plants

Grand Canyon and Colorado River

all the way to the sea. The sea may be rough at the *mouth* — or end — of the river. Or the sea may be calm at the mouth of the river. If it is rough, the sediment will be carried away from the land.

If the sea is calm, the sediment will stay at the mouth of the river. After a long time, it will build up and become an area of land called a *delta*. The soil of a delta is very rich and makes excellent farmland.

Some rivers flow at the bottom of a *canyon*. A canyon is a deep, steep river valley. The Grand Canyon, in Arizona, is one of the largest canyons in the world. It is a mile deep in many places and 277 miles long.

A canyon starts to form when a river erodes dry, rocky land. The water cuts a path that gets deeper and deeper. Millions of years later, the path becomes a canyon.

Niagara Falls with visitors in yellow slickers

Rivers run under the ground too. When they do, they may form *caverns*. A cavern is a hollow place made by water pushing through rock. Some kinds of rock, such as limestone, are very soft. When water flows over this kind of rock, it makes a hole. As time goes by, the hole grows larger and larger until it becomes a cavern.

Sometimes a river runs over hard rock and then over soft rock. When this happens, the water wears away the soft rock faster than it wears away the hard rock. The water shoots and tumbles over the rocks, forming a *rapid*.

As the river erodes the soft rock, the rapid turns into a *waterfall*. The soft rock has all worn away, and now the water drops straight down from the hard rock at the top.

The Niagara River is part of the border between Canada and the United States. The river itself is small, but it creates Niagara Falls, which is one of nature's marvels. The water spills down, down, down — more than 160 feet from top to bottom — in beautiful twin falls.

When water falls a long distance, it lands with great force. This force can be used to power the motors that make electricity for homes and factories. Waterfalls, such as Niagara Falls, are used this way.

Rivers have many uses. People have always settled near rivers, because the rivers provided water to drink and fish to eat. The rivers made the soil rich for growing crops. Before there were cars and planes, people traveled on rivers in boats. They used the rivers to transport goods too. Today, most people do not travel by river, but the river is still used to ship products from one place to another. Barges transport coal, steel, grain, and many other things on their flat decks.

Our rivers are still important to us. Over the years, however, some streams and rivers have become dirty, or *polluted*. Many people are working to make our waters clean again.

Rivers are a powerful force on our planet. They build islands, they carve canyons, and they create waterfalls. We use rivers for energy and transportation too. Swirling and rushing, or gently flowing along, rivers are a beautiful and important part of our earth.

Author

Rae Bains writes under different names and on many different topics. She says, "I write because I love to, and almost everything interests me." Ms. Bains has written articles for adult magazines as well as many books for older children. She and her husband often work together on books under their real names.

Thinking It Over

Comprehension Questions

1. What are some ways in which rivers change the land as they move to the sea?
2. How do most rivers start?
3. What does *erosion* mean?
4. What does *polluted* mean?
5. What are some uses of rivers?
6. What would the earth be like without rivers?

Vocabulary

Use the words below to fill in the blanks in the sentences. You may look back at the article.

marvels   narrow
tumble   unite
curve   trickle

1. Some rivers can _____ like a snake.
2. Many rivers are _____ .
3. Many tiny streams _____ down mountains.
4. In time many streams _____ to form a river.
5. Sometimes rivers _____ over rocks to form a *rapid*.
6. The Niagara River is one of nature's _____ .

Making a Poster

Draw a picture of the Grand Canyon and one of Niagara Falls on poster paper. Below the picture of the Grand Canyon, write how canyons are formed. Below the picture of Niagara Falls, write how waterfalls are made.

THE EMPEROR'S PLUM TREE

adapted from a story by Michelle Nikly
translated by Elizabeth Shub

The emperor is upset because a plum tree
is dying, and his perfect garden will be
perfect no longer. Will finding a new plum
tree make the emperor happy again?

Characters:

Narrator

Emperor of Japan

Emperor's attendants

1st Messenger

2nd Messenger

Ukiyo, *an artist*

Tanka, *his wife,*
  who enjoys writing poetry

Musuko, *their son*

Scene 1

(The setting is the imperial garden in Japan. In the garden are plum trees, peach trees, pines, bamboos, and flowers. The narrator stands near a tree.)

Narrator: Long ago, in the land of the rising sun, there lived an emperor whose garden was beautiful beyond imagination. Each tree, each flower, each stone had its place in the lovely design of the garden. *(Emperor enters garden with attendants)* One morning as the emperor took his daily stroll, he stopped in dismay at a grove of plum trees.

Emperor *(Turning to attendants):* Could that tree near the wall be dying? *(Emperor rushes to tree and feels a twig which breaks off in his hand.)* Oh no! *(Almost sobbing)* This tree will have to be cut down. My perfect garden will be perfect no longer. Oh! How terrible! *(Emperor hurries from garden with hands covering his face. Attendants follow him quickly)*

Narrator: The emperor shut himself up in his palace and refused to go out. Days passed and indoors, the emperor mourned for his garden. At last it was decided that only a plum tree as beautiful as the one that died would restore the garden and make the emperor happy again.

Scene 2

(The setting is a smaller garden. In the garden are the emperor's two messengers, Ukiyo, his wife Tanka, and their son Musuko. There are an easel, paint brushes and pots of paints near Ukiyo. Tanka holds sheets of paper in her hands.)

Narrator: Messengers were sent to search the land and within a day a perfect tree was found in the garden of a painter named Ukiyo.

1st Messenger: Ukiyo, we bring you great honor. Your plum tree has been chosen to take the place of the one that died in the imperial garden.

Ukiyo: Must we part with our plum tree? *(Touching tree's branches)* I love to paint its gnarled branches and starlike flowers.

Tanka *(Holding out to messengers paper in her hand):* And many of the poems I write describe its beauty. Can you find no other plum tree for the imperial garden?

339

2nd Messenger: We have searched the land far and wide. Your plum tree is the only one beautiful enough to be planted in the imperial garden.

Musuko: Please, sirs. I beg that you do not take away our plum tree. It is the home of my friend, the nightingale. I stand at the foot of our tree and speak to her. She replies in her own way, yet we always understand one another as true friends do.

1st Messenger: There is no other tree in the land, Musuko, that can restore the imperial garden and make the emperor happy again.

2nd Messenger: We are sorry, but we have to take this tree.

Ukiyo: Since we must part with our tree, I humbly ask that we keep it one day longer.

Messengers: We see how heartbroken you are. We grant you your desire. (*Messengers leave garden*)

Scene 3

(*The setting is* Ukiyo *and* Tanka's *garden. The messengers have dug up the plum tree. Ukiyo and* Tanka *stand nearby, comforting each other.* Musuko *enters holding a scroll.*)

Musuko (*Running up to one of the messengers*): Please, sir, may I tie this scroll to a branch of the tree?

1st Messenger: How bravely you hold back your tears, Musuko. Yes, you may tie your scroll to the tree. *(Messengers leave with tree. Musuko and his parents stand close together, watching them leave.)*

Scene 4
(The setting is the imperial garden.)

Narrator: Ukiyo's plum tree was replanted in the imperial garden, and the emperor was persuaded to come and see it. *(Emperor enters garden followed by attendants and the two messengers. He stops before plum tree. Everyone watches him anxiously.)*

Emperor *(Turns to messengers and attendants and smiles):* My garden is flawless once again. *(Turning to admire the tree again)* But what is this? A scroll? *(Emperor takes down the scroll and unrolls it.)* It's a drawing of a branch of the plum tree with a nightingale perched on the branch. How wonderfully lifelike it is! And here is a poem:

> At the long day's end,
> when the nightingale flies home,
> what shall I tell her?

(Emperor stands for a long time, deep in thought, in front of the plum tree)

343

Emperor (*Pointing to the messengers*):   Go at once, you two, and bring Ukiyo, Tanka, and Musuko to the palace. (*Messengers* leave. Emperor *looks at plum tree once more, then he leaves the garden, still holding the scroll, followed by his attendants.*)

Scene 5

(*The setting is a room inside the palace.* Emperor *stands while* Ukiyo, Tanka, *and* Musuko *kneel before him.*)

Emperor (*Gently pulling up* Musuko):   My child, I will tell you what to say to your homeless friend. Tell her that her plum tree, borrowed for a day because of the emperor's whim, will be returned to her by the emperor's order.

Ukiyo and Tanka: Your imperial majesty, we want you to . . .

Emperor (*Shaking his head*):   No, no, Ukiyo and Tanka. Do not protest. It seems that my sorrow has been replaced by yours. I could not bear to see this tree each day, knowing that a child lost his friend because of me. This tree belongs in your garden, but before it leaves mine, I have a request.

(To Ukiyo*)* Ukiyo, I ask you to paint my garden, perfect as it is on this day. The death of my plum tree has reminded me that no garden can last forever. One day the peach trees, the pines, and even the bamboos will be no more. But your painting, Ukiyo, will be a lasting reminder of this garden's perfection.

(To Tanka*)* And, Tanka, I ask you to write this story, just as it happened, so that in times to come, children will hear how once the Emperor of Japan learned wisdom from a small boy named Musuko, a nightingale, and a plum tree.

Author

Michelle Nikly, who lives in Europe, first wrote *The Emperor's Plum Tree* in French. After the book was published in France, a well known translator in New York, Elizabeth Shub, retold the story in English so that American children could enjoy it. Another of Ms. Nikly's books that you might enjoy is *The Princess on the Nut*.

Thinking It Over

Comprehension Questions

1. Did finding a new plum tree make the emperor happy again? Why or why not?
2. Where was the new plum tree found?
3. Would you have let the emperor know that he had taken away the nightingale's home? Why or why not?
4. What did the emperor say the death of his plum tree reminded him of? Find and read his exact words on page 346.

Vocabulary

The words below are from the story. Use the words in place of the boldface words in the sentences.

gnarled   **replied**   **heartbroken**
flawless   **stroll**

1. The Emperor took a **walk** in his garden every day.

2. Musuko and his parents were **sad** when their plum tree was taken away.

3. Ukiyo loved to paint the **knotty** branches of the plum tree.

4. Musuko often spoke to the nightingale. The nightingale always **answered** in her own way.

5. The emperor's garden became **perfect** once more when the new plum tree was planted there.

Making a Sign

Pretend that you have an animal friend who lives in the woods. Your friend's home is about to be destroyed. Make a sign to let people know an animal lives there. Write on your sign how the animal will feel about losing its home.

PLUM TREES

by Rankō

So sweet the plum trees smell!
Would that the brush that paints the flower
Could paint the scent as well.

I come to look, and lo,
The plum tree petals scatter down
A fall of purest snow.

Magazine Wrap-up

Story Plots

In "The Mail-Order Monster," "Uncle Somebody and Becky's Birthday," and "The Emperor's Plum Tree," you read about situations that turned out differently from what the main characters had expected. What did Julius, Becky, and the emperor expect, and what actually happened?

Vocabulary

A meaning for each word in the box is listed below the box. Match the words with their meanings.

puzzled	**couch**
timidly	**hornet**
fierce	**unite**
hideous	**marvel**
flawless	**whim**

1. a large insect that can give a painful sting

2. very ugly

3. someone or something that is wonderful

4. a sudden wish

5. confused

6. perfect

7. a piece of furniture that seats two or more people

8. wild and dangerous

9. join

10. acting in a scared way

Main Idea

You have learned that authors do not always include in a paragraph a sentence that tells the main idea. When that happens, you must decide the main idea. Read the paragraph below and write a sentence that tells the main idea of the paragraph.

In the United States, there are many interesting places to spend vacations. Two popular vacation areas are the Grand Canyon and Niagara Falls. Every year many people make vacation trips to the Grand Canyon or to Niagara Falls. Some visitors enjoy driving around the canyon, while others get pleasure from hiking across it. Visitors to Niagara Falls can get excellent views of the falls from observation towers that are 282 to 500 feet high. For more adventurous visitors, there are boats that can take them close to the swirling waters at the base of the falls.

Books to Enjoy

Desert Voices
by Byrd Baylor

A pack rat, a coyote, and eight other desert animals tell how they survive in the dry, rocky land that is their home.

Joseph on the Subway Trains
by Kathleen Benson

On a class trip to New York City, a Brooklyn boy gets on the wrong subway train and has to admit he's lost.

Benjy in Business
by Jean VanLeeuwen

To earn money for a new baseball glove, Benjy goes into business and finds that it is hard work.

The Legend of the Bluebonnet
by Tomie DePaola

A Comanche Indian tale explains how the Texas bluebonnet flowers first come to be.

"In Which Pooh Goes Visiting and Gets Into a Tight Place"

an excerpt from
Winnie-the-Pooh

written by A.A. Milne

illustrated by
E.H. Shepard

A.A. Milne began to write *Winnie-the-Pooh* as he watched his son, Christopher Robin, at play. The real Christopher Robin had a stuffed bear named Winnie-the-Pooh, and Mr. Milne enjoyed writing about Christopher and the bear.

Each chapter is a separate adventure about Christopher Robin's favorite stuffed toys. There are adventures with Piglet, Eeyore, and others. In this chapter, Pooh gets out of a tight spot in an unusual way.

A. A. MILNE

Winnie-the-Pooh

ILLUSTRATED BY
Ernest H. Shepard

In Which

Pooh Goes Visiting and Gets Into a Tight Place

Edward Bear, known to his friends as Winnie-the-Pooh, or Pooh for short, was walking through the forest one day, humming proudly to himself. He had made up a little hum that very morning, as he was doing his Stoutness Exercises in front of the glass: *Tra-la-la, tra-la-la,* as he stretched up as high as he could go, and then *Tra-la-la, tra-la — oh, help! — la,* as he tried to reach his toes. After breakfast he had said it over and over to himself until he had learnt it off by heart, and now he was humming it right through, properly. It went like this:

Tra-la-la, tra-la-la,
Tra-la-la, tra-la-la,
Rum-tum-tiddle-um-tum.
Tiddle-iddle, tiddle-iddle,
Tiddle-iddle, tiddle-iddle,
Rum-tum-tum-tiddle-um.

Well, he was humming this hum to himself, and walking along gaily, wondering what everybody else was doing, and what it felt like, being somebody else, when suddenly he came to a sandy bank, and in the bank was a large hole.

"Aha!" said Pooh. *(Rum-tum-tiddle-um-tum.)* "If I know anything about anything, that hole means Rabbit," he said, "and Rabbit means Company," he said, "and Company means Food and Listening-to Me-Humming and such like. *Rum-tum-tum-tiddle-um.*"

So he bent down, put his head into the hole, and called out:

"Is anybody at home?"

There was a sudden scuffling noise from inside the hole, and then silence.

"What I said was, 'Is anybody at home?'" called out Pooh very loudly.

"No!" said a voice; and then added, "You needn't shout so loud. I heard you quite well the first time."

"Bother!" said Pooh. "Isn't there anybody here at all?"

"Nobody."

see Rabbit getting out the plates and mugs; and when Rabbit said, "Honey or condensed milk with your bread?" he was so excited that he said, "Both," and then, so as not to seem greedy, he added, "But don't bother about the bread, please." And for a long time after that he said nothing . . . until at last, humming to himself in a rather sticky voice, he got up, shook Rabbit lovingly by the paw, and said that he must be going on.

"Must you?" said Rabbit politely.

"Well,"said Pooh, "I could stay a little longer if it — if you — " and he tried very hard to look in the direction of the larder.

"As a matter of fact," said Rabbit, "I was going out myself directly."

"Oh, well, then, I'll be going on. Good-by."

"Well, good-by, if you're sure you won't have any more."

"*Is* there any more?" asked Pooh quickly.

Rabbit took the covers off the dishes, and said, "No, there wasn't."

"I thought not," said Pooh, nodding to himself. "Well, good-by. I must be going on."

So he started to climb out of the hole. He pulled with his front paws, and pushed with his back paws, and in a little while his nose was out in the open again . . . and then his ears . . . and then his front paws . . . and then his shoulders . . . and then ——

"Oh, help!" said Pooh. "I'd better go back."

"Oh, bother!" said Pooh. "I shall have to go on."

"I can't do either!" said Pooh. "Oh, help *and* bother!"

Now by this time Rabbit wanted to go for a walk too, and finding the front door full, he went out by the back door, and came round to Pooh, and looked at him.

"Hallo, are you stuck?" he asked.

"N-no," said Pooh carelessly. "Just resting and thinking and humming to myself."

"Here, give us a paw."

Pooh Bear stretched out a paw, and Rabbit pulled and pulled and pulled. . . .

"*Ow!*" cried Pooh. "You're hurting!"

"The fact is," said Rabbit, "you're stuck."

"It all comes," said Pooh crossly, "of not having front doors big enough."

"It all comes," said Rabbit sternly, "of eating too much. I thought at the time," said Rabbit, "only I didn't like to say anything," said Rabbit, "that one of us was eating too much," said

361

Rabbit, "and I knew it wasn't *me,*" he said. "Well, well, I shall go and fetch Christopher Robin."

Christopher Robin lived at the other end of the Forest, and when he came back with Rabbit, and saw the front half of Pooh, he said, "Silly old Bear," in such a loving voice that everybody felt quite hopeful again.

"I was just beginning to think," said Bear, sniffing slightly, "that Rabbit might never be able to use his front door again. And I should *hate* that," he said.

"So should I," said Rabbit.

"Use his front door again?" said Christopher Robin. "Of course he'll use his front door again."

"Good," said Rabbit.

"If we can't pull you out, Pooh, we might push you back."

Rabbit scratched his whiskers thoughtfully, and pointed out that, when once Pooh was pushed back, he was back, and of course nobody was more glad to see Pooh than *he* was, still there it was, some lived in trees and some lived under-ground, and ——

"You mean I'd *never* get out?" said Pooh.

"I mean," said Rabbit, "that having got *so* far, it seems a pity to waste it."

Christopher Robin nodded.

"Then there's only one thing to be done," he said. "We shall have to wait for you to get thin again."

"How long does getting thin take?" asked Pooh anxiously.

"About a week, I should think."

"But I can't stay here for a *week*!"

"You can *stay* here all right, silly old Bear. It's getting you out which is so difficult."

"We'll read to you," said Rabbit cheerfully. "And I hope it won't snow," he added. "And I say, old fellow, you're taking up a good deal of room in my house — *do* you mind if I use your back legs as a towel-horse? Because, I mean, there they are — doing nothing — and it would be very convenient just to hang the towels on them."

"A week!" said Pooh gloomily. *"What about meals?"*

"I'm afraid no meals," said Christopher Robin, "because of getting thin quicker. But we *will* read to you."

Bear began to sigh, and then found he couldn't because he was so tightly stuck; and a tear rolled down his eye, as he said:

"Then would you read a Sustaining Book, such as would help and comfort a Wedged Bear in Great Tightness?"

So for a week Christopher Robin read that sort of book at the North end of Pooh, and Rabbit hung his washing on the South end . . . and in between Bear felt himself getting slenderer and slenderer. And at the end of the week Christopher Robin said, *"Now!"*

So he took hold of Pooh's front paws and Rabbit took hold of Christopher Robin, and all Rabbit's friends and relations took hold of Rabbit, and they all pulled together. . . .

And for a long time Pooh only said *"Ow!"* . . .

And *"Oh!"* . . .

And then, all of a sudden, he said *"Pop!"* just as if a cork were coming out of a bottle.

And Christopher Robin and Rabbit and all Rabbit's friends and relations went head-over-heels backwards . . . and on the top of them came Winnie-the-Pooh — free!

So, with a nod of thanks to his friends, he went on with his walk through the forest, humming proudly to himself. But, Christopher Robin looked after him lovingly, and said to himself, "Silly old Bear!"

Comprehension Questions

1. Into what kind of a tight place did Pooh
   get himself? What caused him to get there?
   Do you think Pooh will make the same mistake
   if he visits Rabbit again?
2. What clues were there in the story that told
   you Christopher Robin really cared about Pooh?

Author

A. A. Milne was born in London in 1882. He wrote four books about Christopher Robin and his friends. *Winnie-the-Pooh* and *The House at Pooh Corner* are collections of stories. *When We Were Very Young* and *Now We Are Six* are books of poems. Mr. Milne wrote many plays, poems, and stories for adults, but he is remembered most for his Christopher Robin books.

Illustrator

E. H. Shepard first became known as an illustrator for children between 1924 and 1928 when he illustrated *When We Were Very Young* and three other books by A. A. Milne. Since then he has illustrated more than thirty books.

In 1970 Mr. Shepard received the University of Southern Mississippi Children's Collection Medallion for his "outstanding contribution in the field of children's books."

Glossary

This glossary can help you learn the meanings and pronunciations of many words in this book. The meanings of the words as they are used in this book are always given. Often you will also find other common meanings listed.

You can find out the correct pronunciation of any glossary word by using the special spelling and the pronunciation key. The *Full Pronunciation Key* below shows how to pronounce each consonant and vowel in a special spelling. A short form of this key is at the bottom of every left-hand page.

Full Pronunciation Key

Consonant Sounds

b	**bib**	k	cat, **kick**	sh	di**sh**, **sh**ip
ch	**church**	l	**l**id, need**l**e	t	**tight**
d	**deed**	m	a**m**, **m**an	th	pa**th**, **th**in
f	**f**ast, o**ff**	n	**n**o, sudde**n**	*th*	**the**
g	**g**a**g**	ng	thi**ng**	v	ca**v**e, **v**ine
h	**h**at	p	**pop**	w	**w**ith
hw	**wh**ich	r	**r**oa**r**	y	**y**es
j	**judge**	s	mi**ss**, **s**ee	z	**s**ize, **z**ebra
				zh	vi**s**ion

Vowel Sounds

ă	pat	î	dear, fierce	ŭ	cut
ā	pay	ŏ	pot	û	fur
â	air, care	ō	go	yōō	use
ä	father	ô	paw, for	ə	ago, item,
ĕ	pet	oi	boy, noise, oil		pencil, atom
	be	ŏŏ	book		circus
	pit	ōō	boot	ər	butter
	by, pie	ou	cow, out		

...d and reprinted by permission from the *Beginning Dictionary,* copyright © 1979, and ...*erican Heritage School Dictionary,* copyright © 1977, by Houghton Mifflin Company.

A

am•bas•sa•dor (ăm **băs′ə dər**) A person of very high rank who goes to another country to represent his own country or government.

a•re•na (ə **rē′nə**) A covered or open area for sports events or large shows.

as•ton•ish (ə **stŏn′ish**) To surprise greatly.

au•to•mat•ed (ô′tə **māt′ ĭd**) Working with little or no control from others: *That factory is almost completely automated.*

au•to•mat•ic•al•ly (ô′tə **măt′ĭk lē**) Happening without thinking: *The children laughed automatically when they saw the clown.*

a•void (ə **void′**) To keep away from: *Try to leave early so you can avoid the crowds.*

B

bam•boo (băm **boo′**) A tall grass that looks like a tree.

bar•on (**băr′ən**) A nobleman of the lowest rank. During the Middle Ages, a man with lands and a title given by the king.

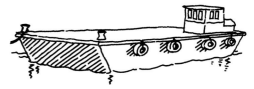

barge (bärj) A boat with a flat bottom used to carry freight on rivers and canals.

be•wil•der•ment (bĭ **wĭl′dər ment**) Confusion.

bluff (blŭf) A steep cliff, hill, or riverbank.

bor•der (**bôr′dər**) The line where one thing ends and another begins.

bump•er (**bŭm′pər**) Something used on a car to soften a blow or protect against being hit or struck.

bush•el (**boosh′əl**) A unit used to measure grain, fruit, vegetables or other dry foods.

bus•tle (**bŭs′əl**) To hurry and move around in a busy and excited way.

C

cat•a•log (**kăt′l ôg′**) A book containing a list of things usually with a short description and in alphabetical order.

cel·e·bra·tion (sĕl′ə brā′ shən) A party or other festive occasion.

co·in·ci·dence (kō ĭn′sĭ dəns) A happening that seems to have been planned but was not.

con·sci·en·tious (kŏn′shē ĕn′shəs) *or* (kŏn′sē-) Done with care: *You have been very conscientious about doing your homework.*

con·serv·a·to·ry (kən sûr′və tôr′ē) *or* (-tōr′ē) A small greenhouse in which plants are grown.

con·ven·ient (kən vēn′yənt) Easy to reach; handy.

cork (kôrk) A stopper for a jar or bottle, made from the bark of a kind of oak tree.

couch (kouch) A piece of furniture usually having a back and seating for two or more persons.

co·zy (kō′zē) Comfortable.

criss·cross (krĭs′krôs′) *or* (krĭs′krŏs′) To mark with or make a pattern of crossing lines: *Animal trails crisscrossed the woods.*

crouch (krouch) To bend low.

crum·ple (krŭm′pəl) **1.** To crush out of shape: *Tracy crumpled a piece of paper.* **2.** To fall down.

D

daw·dle (dôd′l) To take more time than is needed: *Do your homework and don't dawdle.*

de·ceive (dĭ sēv′) To make a person believe something that is not true.

de·pot (dē′pō) A railroad or bus station.

des·ert[1] (dĕz′ərt) A dry region, often covered with sand, having little or no plantlife.

de·sert[2] (dĭ zûrt′) To forsake or leave; abandon.

de·vice (dĭ vīs′) Something that is made or used for a special purpose: *There are many devices for carrying wood.*

ă pat / ā pay / â care / ä father / ĕ pet / ē be / ĭ pit / ī pie / î fierce / ŏ pot / ō go
ô paw, for / oi oil / o͝o book / o͞o boot / ou out / ŭ cut / û fur / *th* the / th thin
hw which / zh vision / ə ago, item, pencil, atom, circus

dis•grace•ful (dĭs **grās′**fəl) Causing shame.

dis•may (dĭs **mā′**) A sudden loss of courage.

diz•zy (**dĭz′**ē) Having a feeling that one is spinning and about to fall.

drear•y (**drîr′**ē) Gloomy, dull.

drows•y (**drou′**zē) Partly asleep; sleepy.

dumb•found (**dŭm′**found′) To make speechless with astonishment: *The judges were dumbfounded by the skater's performance.*

E

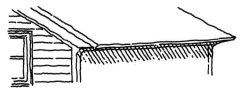

eaves (ēvz) The part of a roof that forms a lower edge and sticks out over the side of a building.

ee•rie *or* **ee•ry** (**îr′**ē) Strange: *An eerie light appeared in the window of the dark house.*

ex•as•per•ate (ĭg **zǎs′**pə rāt′) To annoy; try the patience of: *Ana became exasperated when there were so many changes in the plans.*

ex•pe•ri•ence (ĭk **spîr′**ē əns) A happening, event.

ex•per•i•ment (ĭk **spěr′**ə mənt) Something done to show a fact or find out what might happen: *We did an experiment to show that plants need light to grow.*

ex•pert (**ěk′**spûrt′) A person who knows a lot about something or is very good at it.

ex•plore (ĭk **splôr′**) or (ĭk **splōr′**) To look through a place to find information.

ex•pres•sion (ĭk **sprěsh′**ən) A look that shows a person's mood or feeling.

F

fame (fām) Very well-known; famous.

fash•ion (**fǎsh′**ən) To form; shape: *We fashioned a necklace out of flowers.*

fa•tal (**fāt′**l) Causing death.

fault (fôlt) **1.** A mistake. **2.** Responsibility for something that shouldn't have happened.

fierce (fîrs) **1.** Wild and dangerous: *A fierce animal ran around its cage.* **2.** Very strong; raging: *The fierce rainstorm caused a flood.*

fig·ure·head (**fĭg′**yər hĕd′) **1.** A person who seems to be the leader but has no real power. **2.** A carved figure that is placed on the front of a ship for decoration.

flab·ber·gast (**flăb′**ər găst′) To surprise in a confused way: *Jane forgot that she had entered the contest and was flabbergasted when she won.*

fla·vor (**flā′**vər) Taste: *Onions give a nice flavor to beef stew.*

flaw·less (**flô′**lĭs) Perfect; without error.

flus·ter (**flŭs′**tər) To make excited; confused: *Some people become flustered when they are asked many questions.*

fran·ti·cal·ly (**frăn′**tĭ kăl ĭ) Excitedly with fear or worry: *Randy was searching frantically for his lost wallet.*

freight car (**frāt′**kär) A railway car that carries food or other things: *The farmer sent the vegetables to the market by freight car.*

fre·quent·ly (**frē′**kwənt lē) Happening again and again.

G

gale (gāl) A very strong wind.

gang·plank (**găng′**plangk′) A moveable board that is used for getting on and off a ship.

gape (gāp) *or* (găp) To stare with the mouth open.

gleam (glēm) A bright beam or flash of light.

glit·ter (**glĭt′**ər) To sparkle brightly.

glum·ly (**glŭm′**lē) Saying or doing something in a sad way.

groove (grōōv) A long, narrow cut: *The heavy wheels of the wagon left grooves in the earth.*

grope (grōp) To feel one's way without seeing clearly.

grove (grōv) A group of trees with open ground between them.

guar·an·tee (**găr′**ən tē) To promise: *The salesperson guaranteed that my bed would be delivered on time.*

ă pat / ā pay / â care / ä father / ĕ pet / ē be / ĭ pit / ī pie / î fierce / ŏ pot / ō go
ô paw, for / oi oil / ŏŏ book / ōō boot / ou out / ŭ cut / û fur / th the / th thin
hw which / zh vision / ə ago, item, pencil, atom, circus

H

ham·per (**hăm′**pər) To get in the way of.

har·mo·ny (**här′**mə nē) A balance; pleasing mix of something.

har·ness (**här′**nĭs) A set of leather straps and metal pieces by which an animal is attached to something such as a cart.

haz·y (**hā′**zē) Not clear; confused: *My memory is very hazy about that day.*

heap (hēp) A pile of things lying or thrown together.

hoe (hō) To loosen, cut or dig with a hoe, which is a garden tool that has a flat blade at the end of a long handle.

hon·or·ar·y (**ŏn′**ə rĕr′ē) Given or holding as an honor without having done the usual things for it.

hoot (hoot) To shout or shout at with cries of disapproval: *The crowd hooted when the batter struck out.*

hor·net (**hôr′**nĭt) A large insect that can give a painful sting.

I

im·age (**ĭm′**ĭj) **1.** A copy of a person or thing such as a statue. **2.** A picture of something in the mind.

in·de·pen·dent (**ĭn′**dĭ **pĕn′**dənt) Not controlled by something or someone else.

in·ge·nu·i·ty (**ĭn′**jə **noo′**ĭ tē) *or* (**ĭn′**jə **nyoo′**ĭ tē) Skill in thinking of things; imagination: *Your clay animals show great ingenuity.*

in·her·it (**ĭn hĕr′**ĭt) To receive something from someone after he or she has died.

ir·re·sist·i·ble (**ĭr′**ĭ **zĭs′**tə bəl) Having something that is so strong that a person gives in to it.

isle (īl) A very small island.

J

jas·mine (**jăz′**mĭn) A plant or vine with sweet smelling flowers of yellow and white: *The sweet smell of jasmines filled every room in the house.*

jour·nal (**jûr′**nəl) **1.** A daily record of events. **2.** A magazine or newspaper containing articles about a particular subject.

joust (joust) A fight between two knights on horses.

K

ker·chief (**kûr′**chĭf) A square scarf or piece of cloth worn over the head or around the neck.

ket·tle·drum (**kĕt′**l drŭm′) A large drum with a bowl-shaped body and a top made of sheep or goat skin.

L

lar·der (**lär′**dər) A room where food is kept.

lo·cal (**lō′**kəl) Of a certain area or place

loom (lo͞om) To come into view as large and dangerous: *Dark clouds loomed behind the mountains.*

M

ma·rine (mə **rēn′**) Having to do with the sea.

mar·vel (**mär′**vəl) Someone or something that is wonderful.

mas·cot (**măs′**kŏt′) *or* (**măs′**kət) An animal or person believed to bring good luck.

mill (mĭl) **1.** To move around in a confused way: *A crowd of people milled around outside.* **2.** To crush into very small pieces: *My cousin milled the wheat for the farmer.*

mock (mŏk) False or make-believe.

moist (moist) Slightly wet; damp. *Father cleaned off the table with a moist cloth.*

mo·sa·ic (mō **zā′**ĭk) A picture or design made by fitting together and gluing small pieces of colored tile, glass, stone, or other material.

ă pat / ā pay / â care / ä father / ĕ pet / ē be / ĭ pit / ī pie / î fierce / ŏ pot / ō go
ô paw, for / oi oil / o͝o book / o͞o boot / ou out / ŭ cut / û fur / *th* the / th thin
hw which / zh vision / ə ago, item, pencil, atom, circus

mourn   (môrn) *or* (mōrn) To feel or show sorrow for a death or loss.

must•y   (mŭs′tē) Having a damp, moldy smell.

N

nag   (năg) To pester or annoy.

O

o•gre   (ō′gər) **1.** A giant who eats people.   **2.** A person who is very mean.

op•ti•cal   (ŏp′tĭ kəl) Helping to see: *To see the stars better you can use a special optical instrument called a telescope.*

P

par•a•chute   (păr′ə shoot′) A piece of equipment made of cloth and shaped like an umbrella.

pass•port   (păs′pôrt′) *or* (păs′pōrt′) *or* (păs′pôrt′) *or* (păs′pōrt′) A small paper book that gives permission for a person to travel from one country to another.

pen•man•ship   (pĕn′mən shĭp′) The art or skill of handwriting: *Sue's penmanship is excellent.*

perch   (pûrch) **1.** To land or rest on: *The bird came to perch on my finger.*   **2.** To be in a high position: *The house was perched on the top of the hill.*

per•snick•e•ty   (pər snĭk′ĭ tē) Paying very close attention to detail; fussy.

pest   (pĕst) **1.** A harmful plant or animal.   **2.** An annoying or troublesome person.

pierce   (pîrs) To force through or into.

pi•rate   (pī′rĭt) A person who robs ships at sea.

plan•et   (plăn′ĭt) A heavenly body that moves around the sun: *Earth is one of the planets.*

pla•za   (plăz′ə) *or* (plä′zə) A public square or open area in a town or city.

po•lite•ly   (pə līt′lē) With good manners.

pout   (pout) To push out the lips to show that one is angry or unhappy.

prod•uct   (prŏd′əkt) Something that is made or grown: *Vegetables are farm products.*

prop (prŏp) To keep something from falling by putting something under or against it.

pro·test (prə **tĕst′**) To show strong objection to something.

prow (prou) The pointed front part of a ship or boat; bow.

prowl (proul) To move about slowly and quietly.

R

rack·et[1] (**răk′**ĭt) An oval frame with woven strings used to hit a ball: *Len got a new tennis racket for his birthday.*

rack·et[2] (**răk′**ĭt) A loud, unpleasant noise: *The children made a racket during gym.*

rau·cous (**rô′**kəs) Loud: *A raucous crowd was cheering as the parade went by.*

rel·a·tives (**rĕl′**ə tĭvs) People related by blood or marriage; people who belong to the same family.

re·quest (rĭ **kwĕst′**) Something that is asked for.

re·search (rĭ **sûrch′**) *or* (rē′ sûrch′) The carefully planned study of a subject.

re·store (rĭ **stôr′**) *or* (rĭ **stōr′**) To return to the original.

rhyth·mic (**rĭ***th***′**mĭk) Having a regular pattern of movement, action, or sounds: *I like to hear the rhythmic sounds of drums.*

ri·pen (**rī′**pən) To be fully grown and ready to be used as food.

romp (rŏmp) To race around playfully.

row[1] (rō) A number of persons or things placed next to each other, usually in a straight line.

row[2] (rou) **1.** A noisy quarrel or fight. **2.** A loud noise; racket.

ru·in (**ro͞o′**ĭn) To damage or destroy.

S

sag·gy (**săg′**ē) Sinking down: *This old mattress is saggy.*

sas·sy (**săs′**ē) Fresh: *I got into trouble for my sassy behavior.*

ă pat / ā pay / â care / ä father / ĕ pet / ē be / ĭ pit / ī pie / î fierce / ŏ pot / ō go
ô paw, for / oi oil / o͞o book / o͞o boot / ou out / ŭ cut / û fur / *th* the / th thin
hw which / zh vision / ə ago, item, pencil, atom, circus

sat·is·fac·tion (săt′ĭs făk′ shən) Pleasure that comes from the fulfillment of something.

scone (skōn) *or* (skŏn) A soft, doughy biscuit.

scram (skrăm) To go away at once.

scram·ble (skrăm′bəl) To move quickly, especially by climbing or crawling.

scroll (skrōl) A roll of paper, usually with a message on it.

sham·bles (shăm′bəlz) Disorder: *The yard was left in shambles after the storm.*

shift (shĭft) The period of time that a group of workers work: *Mr. Hill's boss asked him to work the 3:00–11:00 p.m. shift.*

short·stop (shôrt′stŏp′) In baseball, the person who plays between second and third base.

sig·nal (sĭg′nəl) A sign or action that gives information.

sim·i·lar (sĭm′ə lər) Alike but not the same: *A wildcat is similar to but smaller than a lion.*

snug·gle (snŭg′əl) To press close: *Pepíto snuggles under a blanket if he gets cold.*

spear (spîr) To stab with or as if with something sharp like a spear.

sprout (sprout) To begin to grow.

squat (skwŏt) To sit on one's heels, with the knees pulled close to one's chest.

steer[1] (stîr) To direct the course of someone or something: *Carlos steered the car down the hill.*

steer[2] (stîr) A young male domestic cattle raised for beef.

stoop[1] (sto͞op) A forward bending of the head and back: *The clown walked with a stoop.*

stoop[2] (sto͞op) A small staircase leading to a house or building: *Su-Ling likes to sit on the stoop in front of her house.*

stout·ness (stout′nĭs) **1.** Fatness. **2.** Firmness.

stretch·er (strĕch′ər) A kind of bed or cot on which people who are hurt or ill can be carried.

sur·round (sə round′) To be on all sides of; make a circle around.

sus·tain (sə stān′) To hold or keep up.

swift (swĭft) Moving with great speed; fast.

T

tel·e·type·writ·er (tĕl′ə tīp′rī′tər) A special machine that is attached to a phone and spells out messages on paper or on a TV-like screen.

thought·less·ly (thôt′lĭs lē) Without caring about the feelings of others.

thrill (thrĭl) To feel joy or excitement.

tim·id·ly (tĭm′ĭd lē) Shyly; acting in a scared way.

tinge (tĭnj) To color slightly. *The sunset was tinging the sky.*

tour·na·ment (to͝or′nə mənt) *or* (tûr′nə mənt) A contest among several persons or teams in which they compete until there is a winner.

tow·el-horse (tou′əl hôrs) Something made of wood on which to hang towels.

trop·i·cal (trŏp′ĭ kəl) **1.** Of, like, or found in the areas of the earth that are near the equator. **2.** Hot and humid.

U

u·nique (yo͞o nēk′) Being the only one of its kind: *Alaska is unique because it is the largest state in the United States.*

u·nite (yo͞o nīt′) To bring together or join so as to form a whole; make one.

un·rav·el (ŭn răv′əl) To undo something that is knitted.

V

vol·un·teer (vŏl′ən tîr′) To give or offer something without being asked.

W

wad·dle (wŏd′l) To walk with short steps that sway the body from side to side, just as a duck does.

ă pat / ā pay / â care / ä father / ĕ pet / ē be / ĭ pit / ī pie / î fierce / ŏ pot / ō go
ô paw, for / oi oil / o͝o book / o͞o boot / ou out / ŭ cut / û fur / *th* **the** / th **thin**
hw **wh**ich / zh vision / ə **a**go, item, pencil, atom, circus

ware·house (wâr′hous′) A large building where things are stored.

warp (wôrp) In weaving, the threads that run up and down.

wa·ter·proof (wô′tər proof′) *or* (wŏt′ər proof′) Capable of keeping water from coming through.

web (wĕb) A design of thin threads or lines that looks like a spider's web.

wedge (wĕj) To push or force into a small place.

weft (wĕft) In weaving, the threads that run across the threads that run up and down.

wharves (hwôrvz) *or* (wôrvz) Places where boats and ships tie up to load or unload.

whim (hwĭm) *or* (wĭm) A sudden wish; idea.

whiz (hwĭz) *or* (wĭz) To move quickly with a humming or buzzing sound: *The train was a blur as it went whizzing by.*

wis·dom (wĭz′dəm) Knowing what to do, and what is good and bad, and right and wrong.

wit (wĭt) The ability to think clearly: *You must keep your wits about you while driving during a bad storm.*

wreck (rĕk) What is left of something that is destroyed: *My car was a total wreck after it was hit.*

Z

zin·ni·a (zĭn′ē ə) A garden plant with showy, variously colored flowers: *Our zinnias won first prize at the annual spring flower show.*

Reading Helps

Here are some things to remember when you meet a new word.

1. Use the letter sounds and the context—the meanings of nearby words and sentences.

   During Ed's first weeks in school, he was very shy. As time went on, he became less **timid,** and now he has many friends.

   timid - shy, afraid

2. Sometimes a word is made up of a *prefix* or *suffix* added to a base word. Use the meanings of the base word and its prefix or suffix to figure out the meaning of the new word.

   She **retold** the story because we liked it.

Prefix	Base Word	Meaning
re-	told	told again

   My cat has long, **silky** fur.

Base Word	Suffix	Meaning
silk	-y	like silk

3. Sometimes you can figure out a new word by dividing it into syllables and saying each syllable as if it were a word by itself.

   - If a word has *two* consonants between two vowels, try dividing the word between the consonants.

market	mar ket
hermit	her mit

   - If a word has *one* consonant between two vowels, try dividing the word before the consonant, using the *long* sound for the *first* vowel.

flavor	fla vor

   - If the word does not make sense, try dividing it *after* the first consonant, using the *short* sound for the first vowel.

level	lev el

4. If you do not know what a word means or how it should be pronounced, look up the word in the Glossary or in a dictionary.

Writing Helps

Step One
Choose a story idea.

Think about what you are going to tell in your story.

- Who will the characters be?
- What things are going to happen in your story?
- How will the story end?

Step Two
Write your story.

Now write your ideas down on paper. Just write; you will have a chance to make changes later.

Step Three
Revise your story.

Revise means to make changes that will improve your story.
Use these questions to help you:

- Does your story have a good beginning?
- Does each sentence tell something that is important to the story?
- Will your sentences keep people interested in your story?
- Does your story have a good ending?

Step Four
Proofread your story.

Proofread means to read over and correct mistakes.
Use these questions to help you:

- Did you use capital letters correctly?
- Did you use punctuation correctly?
- Are all the words spelled correctly?
- Did you indent all paragraphs?

Step Five
Make a final copy.

Prepare a neat, clean copy of the story that will be easy for others to read.

Continued from page 2.
"The Fastest Quitter in Town," adapted from *The Fastest Quitter in Town*, by Phyllis Green. Copyright © 1972 by Phyllis Green. Reprinted by permission of Addison-Wesley, Reading, Massachusetts.

"Hannah Is a Palindrome," abridged and adapted from *Hannah Is a Palindrome* (pages 94–109) by Mindy Warshaw Skolsky. Text copyright © 1980 by Mindy Warshaw Skolsky. Reprinted by permission of Harper & Row, Publishers, Inc.

"Harald and the Giant Knight," adapted from *Harald and the Giant Knight*, by Donald Carrick. Copyright © 1982 by Donald Carrick. Reprinted by permission of Ticknor & Fields/Clarion Books, a Houghton Mifflin Company.

"The Library," by Barbara A. Huff, from *The Random House Book of Poetry*, edited by Jack Prelutsky. Copyright © 1983. Reprinted by permission of the author.

"The Mail-Order Monster," adapted from *The Monster in the Mail Box*, by Sheila Gordon. Copyright © 1978 by Sheila Gordon. Reprinted by permission of the publisher, E. P. Dutton, Inc. and Lescher & Lescher, Ltd.

"Miss Rumphius," adapted from *Miss Rumphius*, Story and Pictures by Barbara Cooney. Copyright © 1982 by Barbara Cooney Porter. Published in Great Britain by Julia MacRae Books. Reprinted by permission of Viking Penguin Inc.

"My Grandmother Tells Me," title changed from *Along Sandy Trails*, by Ann Nolan Clark. Text Copyright © 1969 by Ann Nolan Clark. Reprinted by permission of Viking Penguin Inc.

"Owney, the Traveling Dog," adapted from *Owney the Traveling Dog* by Lynn Hall. Copyright © 1977 by Lynn Hall. Reprinted by permission of Garrard Publishing Co., Champaign, Illinois.

"Plum Trees," by Rankō, from *A Year of Japanese Epigrams* by William N. Porter. Copyright © 1911. Reprinted by permission of Oxford University Press.

"Ramón and the Pirate Gull," adapted from *Ramón and the Pirate Gull* by Robert Barry. Copyright © 1971. Reprinted by permission of McGraw-Hill Book Company.

"Sea Shopping," by Bette Killion. Copyright © 1982 by the National Wildlife Federation. Reprinted from the August 1982 issue of *Ranger Rick*, by permission of the publisher, the National Wildlife Federation.

"Thinking," by Felice Holman, from *At the Top of My Voice and Other Poems*. Text copyright © 1970 by Felice Holman. Reprinted by permission of Charles Scribner's Sons.

"A Toad for Tuesday," adapted from pp. 22–44, 55–64 of *A Toad for Tuesday* by Russell E. Erickson. Text Copyright © 1974 by Russell E. Erickson. Reprinted by permission of Lothrop, Lee & Shepard Books (A Division of William Morrow & Company).

"Travel," by Edna St. Vincent Millay, from *Collected Poems*, Harper & Row. Copyright © 1921, 1948 by Edna St. Vincent Millay. Reprinted by permission of Norma Millay Ellis.

"What Makes a Bird a Bird?," by May Garelick. Copyright © 1973. Originally appeared in *Cricket* magazine. Adapted and reprinted by permission of the author.

"Winnie-the-Pooh," from *Winnie-the-Pooh* and *The House at Pooh Corner*, by A.A. Milne, illustrated by Ernest H. Shepard. Copyright © 1926, 1928 by E.P. Dutton, renewed, 1954, 1956 by A.A. Milne. Reprinted by permission of the publisher, E. P. Dutton, Inc. and Methuen Children's Books. Line illustrations by E.H. Shepard © under the Bairn Convention, reproduced by permission of Curtis Brown, Ltd., London.

"Wonders of Rivers," from *Wonders of Rivers* by Rae Bains. Copyright © 1982 by Troll Associates. Reprinted by permission of Troll Associates, Mahwah, New Jersey.

"Words in Our Hands," adapted from *Words in Our Hands* by Ada B. Litchfield. Text copyright © 1980 by Ada B. Litchfield. Reprinted by permission of Albert Whitman & Company.

Grateful acknowledgment is made for permission to reprint and adapt material from the *Beginning Dictionary*, copyright © 1979 by Houghton Mifflin Company, and from *The American Heritage School Dictionary*, copyright © 1977 by Houghton Mifflin Company.

Credits

Cover and title page illustrated by Kathy Mitchell
Magazine openers illustrated by Thierry Chatelain

Illustrators: 6–7 Thierry Chatelain **10–28**
Jeremy Guitar **29** Tom Powers **41** Robert
Blake **42–43** Anthony Accardo **44–59** Larry
Raymond **62** Robert Blake **65–76** Buena
Johnson **77** Donna Diamond **78–91** Michael
Adams **94–109** Cherie Wyman **110–111** An-
thony Accardo **112–137** Doug Cushman **140–
141** Thierry Chatelain **144–161** Donald Carrick
162–163, 181 Anthony Accardo **182–194**
Higgins Bond **195** D. J.Simison **210–211**
Anthony Accardo **212–223** Barbara Cooney
224–225 Carol Schwartz **240–249** Kristina
Rodanas **254–255** Thierry Chatelain **258–276**
Winfield Coleman **277** Julie Downing **278–279**
Anthony Accardo **304–305** Anthony Accardo
306–323 Mary Beth Schwark **335–348** Michelle
Nikly **349** Pat Wong **352–367** Ernest H.
Shepard **368–379** George M. Ulrich

Photographers: 30 Michal Heron
32 © John Moss/After Image **34** David K.
Smith **35** The Granger Collection, New York
34, 36, 38 David K. Smith **39** © Pam
Hasegawa **40** David K. Smith **64** Jeffrey Mark
Dunn **92–93** The National Theatre of the Deaf
164–180 Ralph Mercer **196** © Ellis Herwig/
The Picture Cube **199** Michal Heron **200** © Dr.
E. R. Degginger **201** (top) © Stephen Dalton/
Animals Animals **201** (bottom) © Jane Burton/
Bruce Coleman Inc. **202** (top) © Hans
Reinhard/Bruce Coleman Inc. **202** (bottom),
203 (top) © Dr. E. R. Degginger
203 (bottom) © Stephen Dalton/Animals
Animals **204** (top) © F. V. Unverhau/Animals
Animals **204** (bottom) © Dr. E. R. Degginger
205 © Animals Animals **206** (top) © Dr. E. R.
Degginger **206** (bottom) © Leonard Lee Rue
III **207** (top) © Zig Leszczvynski/Animals
Animals **207** (bottom) © Laura Riley/Bruce
Coleman Inc. **208** © Bill Binzen **230**
© Bob Hahn/Taurus Photos **232** Grant Heil-
man Photography **233** Barry L. Ruck/Grant
Heilman Photography **234** (top) © Dr. E. R.
Degginger **234** (bottom) Patti Murray/

EARTH SCENES **235** © Zig Leszczvynski/
Animals Animals **236** (top) © Breck Plant
236 (bottom) © Zig Leszczvynski/Animals
Animals **237** © Dr. E. R. Degginger **279**
© Mike Malyszko/Stock Boston **278** ©
Leonard Lee Rue III **283** Michal Heron
285 © Robert Crandall Associates, Inc.
286–303 James L. Ballard/Ligature Inc. **326**
Ian Berry/Magnum **327** © Taurus Photos
328–331 Grant Heilman Photography **332**
Tom Hollyman/Photo Researchers, Inc.